ROBERT BLY, 1985
Photograph courtesy of Ann Leavy

Robert Bly

By Richard P. Sugg

Florida International University

Twayne Publishers
A Division of G.K. Hall & Co. • Boston

Robert Bly

Richard P. Sugg

Copyediting supervised by Lewis DeSimone
Book production by Elizabeth Todesco
Book design by Barbara Anderson

Typeset in 11 pt. Garamond
by P&M Typesetting, Inc., Waterbury, Connecticut

Printed on permanent/durable acid-free paper
and bound in the United States of America

Library of Congress Cataloging in Publication Data

Sugg, Richard P.
   Robert Bly.

   (Twayne's United States authors series; TUSAS 513)
   Bibliography: p. 152
   Includes index.
   1. Bly, Robert—Criticism and interpretation.
I. Title. II. Series.
PS3552.L9Z88   1986   811'.54   86-9934
ISBN 0-8057-7480-7

Contents

About the Author

Richard P. Sugg is professor of American literature and humanities at Florida International University, the Miami campus of the State University System of Florida. He has taught previously at the University of Florida and the University of Kentucky. His books include *Hart Crane's "The Bridge": A Description of Its Life* and *Appreciating Poetry*. He has published essays on Walt Whitman, Hart Crane, Robert Bly, Ernest Hemingway, Thomas Gray, and Joseph Conrad.

Preface

Robert Bly is among the best American poets since 1945. Without question, he has been the most influential upon his own and younger generations. Not only through his many books of poetry and translations, as well as his acclaimed poetry readings, but also through his lifelong participation in the more public worlds of literary and social criticism, Bly's lifework has helped to redefine for the postwar generations the role of the American poet. His first book, *Silence in the Snowy Fields* (1962), was highly praised for its innovative wedding of European and Latin American surrealist techniques to native American themes. Bly's second book, *The Light around the Body* (1967), won the prestigious National Book Award; its poetry about the Vietnam war not only crystallized the issues and emotions of that momentous event in American history, but also forcefully demonstrated that poetry could have an important voice in the national dialogue. *Sleepers Joining Hands* (1973) traced the poet's midlife movement away from political subjects to psychological concerns. During the seventies Bly adopted, and helped popularize, the prose poem form in order to explore better the relationship between man, nature, and the elemental, divine instinctuality in the universe. In *The Morning Glory* (1975), *This Body Is Made of Camphor and Gopherwood* (1979), and *This Tree Will Be Here for a Thousand Years* (1979), Bly's increasingly spiritual impulse came to fruition, in what is the most impressive religious poetry from an American poet during the past twenty years. Bly's anthology *News of the Universe* (1980) reinterpreted the Western literary tradition of the past 400 years to demonstrate the universality of his spiritual themes. In *The Man in the Black Coat Turns* (1981) the aging poet struggled with the perennial question of fate versus free will in the evolution of his psyche, of his family, and of the family of man. Bly's work in *Loving a Woman in Two Worlds* (1985) suggests that his poetic vigor remains undiminished. This sketch of the poet's achievement, whose abundance includes more than thirty books of poetry and translation, demonstrates why Robert Bly's influence upon American poets should remain long-lived and pervasive.

This study of Robert Bly's achievement proceeds along three levels. As I believe it must, it starts from an extensive critical survey and analysis of the poetry to date, focusing especially on poems from Bly's *Selected Poems* and drawing frequently upon his criticism and interviews to interpret and illuminate the work. Individual images and poems become clearer when considered in the context of Bly's carefully arranged books; indeed, there are recurring Bly symbols, such as the "snowy fields" of his first book, whose most comprehensive context is nothing less than his collected works. Hence any study must start from a base of extensive, close readings of the poems, in order to amplify the resonances of the images and trace the metamorphoses of the themes which are so integral to Bly's poetics.

The study further broadens its scope by developing each chapter around a larger literary issue. Bly is especially receptive to this strategy, since both as poet and critic he consciously addresses many of the central issues of his time. Chapter 1 uses Bly's criticism to orient the reader to particular issues and important stages in Bly's literary life. Chapter 2 analyzes the poetry of *Silence in the Snowy Fields* in the context of the fifties' literary debate between proponents of the "deep image" and the confessional poets and New Critics. Chapter 3 treats *The Light around the Body* in terms of the literary debate about the validity of political poetry. And chapter 4 uses *Sleepers Joining Hands* to formulate the issues surrounding the poet's use of Jungian, archetypal imagery and themes. Chapter 5 elucidates Bly's attempt to revive a religious spirit toward nature, and to reorient literary history around that spirit, in terms that can appeal to postindustrial man. Finally, chapter 6 discusses Bly's search for a valid archetypal symbolism for immortality through generationality in his most recent poetry about his personal and ancestral life. This strategy provides the reader with relevant historical-critical contexts for appreciating Bly's poetry.

Finally, this study attempts to establish a continuity for Bly's career, in the midst of its diversity, in terms of his fidelity to the Jungian theme of "the inward road," the lifelong journey through individuation to integration which both Bly and Jung believe to be the inherent method and goal of personality development. My thesis, gently argued, is that Bly's work should be read and understood in terms of his pervasive commitment to themes and even imagery best described by Jungian psychology. Seen in this light, Bly's poetry proves to be not only eminently lucid but also powerfully persuasive in its faithful articulation of the poet's lifelong psychospiritual impulse.

Preface

I would like to thank the staff of the F.I.U. library, especially Toni Baker Downs, Judy Baran, and Charlie Easton, for help in gathering material for this book. Thanks also to the University of Virginia for granting me a courtesy appointment for the year during which this study was begun, and to F.I.U. for financially supporting that sabbatical year. Several colleagues deserve acknowledgment for various contributions to this project, including Tucker Arnold, Ken Henley, Ramon Mendoza, Richard Messer, Joyce Peterson, and Fernando Gonzalez-Regiosa. Allen Tilley deserves a special mention for his extensive comments on the manuscript. Frank Burke and Bob Nadeau were, as always, supportive. Kathleen O'Brien provided the best Bly anecdote, and Shakespeare & Company, an amiable Paris bookstore, provided a very scarce English-keyboard typewriter when the index had to be typed. Finally, invoking the spirit of generationality and of family, I dedicate this book to my wife Ellen and our son Pete.

Richard P. Sugg

Florida International University

Acknowledgments

Excerpts from the following works are reprinted by permission of Harper & Row, Publishers, Inc.: *The Light around the Body: Poems by Robert Bly,* copyright 1959, 1960, 1961, 1962, 1963, 1964, 1965, 1966, 1967 by Robert Bly; *Sleepers Joining Hands* copyright 1973 by Robert Bly; *This Body is Made of Camphor and Gopherwood,* copyright 1977 by Robert Bly; *This Tree Will Be Here for a Thousand Years,* copyright 1979 by Robert Bly.

Excerpts from *The Man in the Black Coat Turns,* copyright 1981 by Robert Bly, are reprinted by permission of Doubleday & Company, Inc.

Lines from "Under Ben Bulben," from *Collected Poems of W. B. Yeats,* copyright 1940 by George Yeats, copyright renewed 1968 by Bertha Georgie Yeats, Michael Butler Yeats, and Anne Yeats, are reprinted by permission of Macmillan Publishing Company. Excerpts from *The Collected Poems of Wallace Stevens,* copyright 1923, renewed 1951, by Wallace Stevens, are reprinted by permission of Alfred A. Knopf, Inc.

Excerpts from the following are reprinted by permission of Robert Bly: *Silence in the Snowy Fields,* copyright 1962 by Robert Bly; "Leaping Up into Political Poetry"; letter to Richard P. Sugg; the *Fifties, Sixties, and Seventies.*

Chronology

1926   Robert Elwood Bly born 23 December to Norwegian-American farmers in Madison, Minnesota.

1944   Joins Navy, sees Chicago and Florida. Meets men interested in poetry; reads Sandburg and Whitman.

1946–1950   College at St. Olaf's (one year) and Harvard (three years). Chooses vocation of poet; delivers class poem.

1951–1953   Poor and alone in New York City, reading Rilke and writing. Psychic experience of "the inward road."

1954–1956   Moves west. Earns M.A. at University of Iowa writing program. Marries Carolyn McLean. Returns to Minnesota farm.

1956–1957   Fulbright award to Norway. Discovers European and Latin American surrealists. Changes poetic style.

1958   Founds literary magazine the *Fifties* (later, the *Sixties* and the *Seventies*). Meets James Wright.

1961   *Twenty Poems of Georg Trakl,* translated with James Wright.

1962   *Silence in the Snowy Fields,* Bly's first book.

1966   National organizer of antiwar poetry readings. Edits *A Poetry Reading against the Vietnam War* and *Forty Poems Touching on Recent American History.*

1967   *The Light around the Body;* wins National Book Award (1968).

1968   *Twenty Poems of Pablo Neruda,* translated with James Wright.

1969   *Tennessee Poetry Journal* publishes special Bly issue. Reads Jung, and Erich Neumann's *The Great Mother.*

1971   *Neruda & Vallejo: Selected Poems,* translated with James Wright and John Knoepfle.

1973   *Sleepers Joining Hands,* includes "The Teeth Mother Naked at Last" (1970); *Lorca & Jiminez: Selected Poems.*

1975 *The Morning Glory,* includes "The Point Reyes Poems" (1974). Organizes First Annual Conference on the Great Mother.

1977 *The Kabir Book;* conference on the Great Mother and the New Father.

1979 *This Body is Made of Camphor and Gopherwood; This Tree Will Be Here For a Thousand Years.*

1980 Marries Ruth Ray. *News of the Universe: Poems of Twofold Consciousness; Talking All Morning.* Death of Bly's former colleague and friend, the poet James Wright.

1981 *The Man in the Black Coat Turns; Selected Poems of Rainer Maria Rilke,* translated by Bly.

1982 Bly's Mother Conference becomes Conference on Form.

1983 *The Eight Stages of Translation.*

1985 *Selected Poems of Antonio Machado,* translated by Bly. *Loving a Woman in Two Worlds.* "Robert Bly's Eleventh Annual Conference of the Great Mother and The New Father: The Orpheus Myth," featuring Joseph Campbell, Ursula K. LeGuin, William Stafford, and the Jungian analyst Linda Leonard, held in Mendocino, California.

1986 *Selected Poems.*

Chapter One

The Geography of
Bly's Imagination

Robert Bly has made his home for the last quarter century in a locale worthy of a hermit—the isolate landscape of western Minnesota, near Madison; yet Bly is perhaps the best known of all contemporary American poets. His fame is based not only upon his poetry, but also upon his formidable presence on the American literary scene—projected through unforgettable performance-readings, numerous essays, frequent interviews, and most broadly through his influential journal the *Fifties* (later titled the *Sixties* and the *Seventies*). Bly's activist role as a man of letters has always complemented, and during some periods seemed to overshadow, his poetry; academic critics, especially, once seemed temperamentally repelled by Bly's youthful fame and anti-establishment attitudes. Furthermore, the style of involvement of the sixties, of which Bly was exemplar, is now out of favor. Charles Altieri accurately describes poetry's "dominant mode"[1] in the eighties, a widespread style that has achieved institutionalized power through the many creative writing programs in American universities, as favoring noninvolvement in politics and society and avoidance of intellectual concepts. Finally, the great variety of Bly's literary activities almost ensures that his reputation will always be based on judgments of many things besides his poetry: "Bly has touched upon and often irritated virtually every poet and every issue in contemporary poetry in at least one of his roles: editor, satirist, theorizer, organizer, translator, regionalist, prizewinner, and iconoclast."[2] Still, poets such as Galway Kinnell count Robert Bly among the two or three most important of his generation. And if influence upon others were the sole criterion, then Bly would stand alone. Bly's poetry has had a powerful and pervasive influence on a whole generation. The poet William Matthews expressed a commonly held sentiment when he declared in 1969 that "Bly has come to dominate American poetry. Young poets refer to him either with rancor or like Sunday golf-

ers talking about Arnold Palmer."³ Bly's prose receives equally
generous praise: "It is nearly impossible to overemphasize the importance of Bly's criticism. . . . there has been nothing so interesting or
influential since Ezra Pound began sending reviews to *Poetry*."⁴ Such
statements could not apply to any other poet of Bly's generation.

But quite apart from Bly's influence on his peers, there is the question of the relevance of Bly's criticism for his own poetry. It is wrong
to read the poetry as primarily an adjunct to the criticism, though
such a danger is always present with essays so original, so powerful,
as Bly's are. But it is equally myopic to ignore altogether a body of
criticism so extensive and so clearly self-referential, even autobiographical, as Bly's. Matthews speaks to the reader's necessary balancing of life and work in understanding Bly's poetry, and captures as
well the delicacy of that relationship, in his remark that "poets who
are also critics write not only about other poems but always, in an
elaborate code, about their own—both those they have written and
those they aspire to write."⁵ Bly's life as a man of letters, especially
the ideas developed in his prose writings, can illuminate many aspects
of his poetry, but only for the reader who has a familiarity with both.
Indeed, a cursory reading of Bly's criticism often appears to contradict
the evidence of the poems, their deepest impulses, even while it may
accurately describe many of their superficial characteristics. For example, it is doubtful whether anyone would have believed that the author of the quiet poems of the inner life of *Silence in the Snowy Fields*
could express successfully that same inwardness refigured through an
ironic, political mask in the work of *The Light around the Body*—that
the two voices, one private and the other public, could be so identifia-
bly, authentically Bly's, in spite of their ostensible differences of subject and tone! Similarly, it is indeed "an elaborate code" that attempts
to reconcile Bly's call for a poetry written far from the centers of ambition in business and the universities with his many readings at campuses across the country, not only on behalf of American Writers
Against the Vietnam War during the sixties, but since then as well.

But Bly himself has written forcefully for the past twenty-five years
against the New Critics' argument enforcing the separation and com-
partmentalizing of a poet's life and work, attacking it as an artificial
and debilitating aestheticism imposed on American criticism by
narrow-minded academics. Bly praises the belief in the essential unity
of a poet's life and work that he cites an an enduring characteristic of
both the criticism and the literature of Europe and South America.

Further, Bly's own poetry frequently includes direct references to both his public and his personal life, so that in effect he invites the reader to entangle the life and work, especially in the long autobiographical poem "Sleepers Joining Hands" and the poems that follow. Any comprehensive account of Robert Bly's work must utilize significant materials from other areas of his life, especially those to which he himself granted a special status by reworking and incorporating them into his poetry.

There are four periods of his life prior to 1962, when he published his first book of poems, *Silence in the Snowy Fields,* that especially influenced his development. These time/places have all been designated by Bly as special regions in the geography of his imagination, origins from which his poetic imagination developed, home places to which it can and does return throughout his career. The aim of this chapter will be to reveal the enduring significance for Bly's poetry of these four influential periods. This task will involve not only explaining how poetic images and themes prominent throughout Bly's career find their initial inspiration in these early periods. It must also convey a sense of the fluid interaction over a lifetime of the four periods; for they gradually become for both reader and poet inextricably identified with four different areas of Bly's own psyche as it evolves through his lifetime. A final, important purpose of approaching the material of Bly's early career in this way is to honor Bly's belief that the psychological, inward significance of events is as important as the meaning attached to their more visible external causes and manifestations. Bly's most enduring poetic theme is the importance of the inward journey through the psyche, and his entire career illustrates a continuing devotion to exploring the geography of that dark region, and to understanding the inward causes of external events. Thus it is useful for the reader to understand as orientation points on the map of Bly's poetic imagination these four influences that may be labeled, for convenience, Minnesota, Harvard/New York, Norway, and the *Fifties.* Many associations of image, theme, and style originate from and cluster around these points of origin and help to define the major characteristics of Bly's poetic career.

Minnesota

Robert Bly was born in Minnesota in 1926, the son of second generation Norwegian immigrants. He grew up on a farm, for a time attended a one-room school, and when he was of age during World War II joined the Navy. Bly wrote an important essay about his childhood, "Being a Lutheran Boy-god in Minnesota," describing his Minnesota as a society of "maddening cheerfulness"[6] where everyone lived by repressing doubt, anger, and even the concept of an unconscious side of human personality. Bly's poems scarcely ever speak directly of the people of Minnesota (though "Afternoon Sleep" in *Silence* is a beautiful exception). Rather, in Bly's imagination Minnesota is weather and terrain carefully observed and gradually composed into a symbolic landscape. Bly's symbolic Minnesota always remains vividly physical, but it comes to express inferentially the landscape of the soul through which runs the "inward road" Bly has walked during his entire life. Further, Bly's symbolic Minnesota, even in his poems of deepest solitude, always carries the aura, however faint, of the essentially human character of a struggle to reclaim the socially repressed, creative unconscious life that lies buried in the people Bly seldom writes about.[7]

In a recent book, *The Man in the Black Coat Turns,* Bly has written poems about his own family, including his ancestors. But even there he speaks of the family members in terms of the archetypal configurations of mother-father-child, or of ancestral evolution, rather than in terms of personal memories of familiar people. Deborah Baker's interesting essay, "Making a Farm: A Literary Biography," argues that for a long time Bly was driven by a particular "wound"[8] he received from his parents, especially from his mother. But the evidence of the recent poetry, as well as Bly's own testimony, is that his wound "is related to an indifferent relationship with his father."[9] Regardless, Bly presents the conflicts between generations as one of numerous examples of the stress accompanying any evolutionary passage between stages of personality development (Bly might prefer the neo-Jungian James Hillman's term "soul-making"[10] here); Bly's conflicts are always defined as archetypal, or paradigmatic, rather than social or individual. Even calling himself a "Luthern boy-god" allows him to subordinate his personal childhood experience to the more universal categories of sociology and history, to identify himself as just another example of a child suffering under the flawed educational curriculum that was imposed on all children after the Protestant Reformation capitulated to rationalism and expunged from its view of human nature any reference to a usable unconscious life.

Thus Bly's Minnesota is neither a beloved nor hated place in his personal memory; it is a frontier his imagination can explore and use to reclaim the inner landscape, the unconscious life that parents and society had earlier denied. When, at the age of thirty-one, he returned to Minnesota in 1958 to live on his father's farm, it was neither to redress old social wrongs by taking his rightful, adult role in society, nor to heal old personal wounds by taking a man's place in his family. Rather, Bly returned to establish a psychological home base, a starting point for a life as a poet on a journey down "the inward road"[11] of self-discovery. The major subject of his work has always been the inward, psychological life of the individual, a choice that had its origins years before Bly's return to Minnesota, during his Harvard/New York period.

Harvard/New York

After World War II, Bly used the G.I. Bill to attend Harvard University. There for the first time he encountered a group of people who worked at being poets, including Donald Hall, Adrienne Rich, and John Ashbery.[12] Bly now credits this community with confirming him in his decision to become a poet. Though he has often attacked the university community, both the creative writing programs that have proliferated throughout the country and the writer-professors who staff them, in recent years Bly has spoken affectionately of his undergraduate days as a student and member of the *Harvard Advocate* staff. Bly even got the prize given annually by the *Advocate* for the year's best poem. Its subject, the frontier Indians, looked forward to the psychological themes of American poetry in the sixties;[13] but its style looked backward, to Robert Lowell.

The evolution of Bly's style through the Harvard/New York period, which is perhaps best traced through Bly's poems in the *Paris Review*,[14] reflects a development common to poets of Bly's generation. Indeed, in many important ways Bly's career is a synecdoche for the development of American poetry from the early fifties to the present. The first problem all American poets of the sixties generation faced was how to work through and to break away from the oppressive style and themes of Anglo-American modernism, a movement that had dominated American literary sensibilities for forty years. The second problem for the sixties poets was to discover not only a subject suit-able for the individual (such as Bly's "inwardness"), but also new sty-listic models (Bly's were the European and Latin American surrealists) to help them break free from the imposing legacy of T. S. Eliot. With a strong model for breaking away from the stranglehold of modernism, the young poets could finally bring contemporary poetry into a pluralistic world, one favorable to a variety of styles and sub-jects that Anglo-American modernism had frowned upon, especially political subjects and associational styles.

Bly's evolution occurred in conjunction with several formative ex-periences which generated a cluster of associated themes and images that remain important throughout his career. If the Harvard years were Bly's introduction to the vocation of a poet, then the years in New York immediately after Harvard were the time of Robert Bly's testing the strength of his vocation, as well as of his discovering the lifelong subject of his work. New York, Bly feels, taught him the need for a poet to pursue his "solitude,"[15] to develop his vocation in relative isolation from others. Bly speaks of it in poems and inter-views with the greatest reverence and respect. He lived a life of ex-treme poverty and loneliness there, doing little but reading and writing; but he discovered in New York what to this day remains the most important and enduring theme in his work: the necessity of traveling the path of inwardness, of growing as a person by exploring and lifting into the light of consciousness the dark, unconscious side of his psyche.

Bly's poetry returns to this most crucial of its formative influences again and again. It is present in such an early poem as "After Work-ing" in *Silence*. The most important description occurs in "The Night Journey in the Cooking Pot," a lengthy section of "Sleepers Joining Hands." There he describes his almost mystical discovery of the in-ward road: "I felt the road first in New York, in that great room / reading Rilke in the womanless loneliness. / . . . the inward path I still walk on"(*S*, 59). And thirty years later, in *The Man in the Black Coat Turns*, the motif recurs in the Zen koan that begins the poem "The Grief of Men." Certainly, Bly's entire poetic career offers ample evidence of the importance of this experience. What New York symbolizes for Bly, then, is precisely this psychospiritual imperative to pursue the vocation of a poet of "the inward road," to explore con-sciously the unconscious life that lies hidden behind, to borrow

Jung's title for his own spiritual autobiography, "memories, dreams, reflections."[16]

Norway

In 1956 Bly won a Fulbright award to study in Norway, home of his ancestors, and there he made a discovery that came to symbolize for him the third of his important origins and to provide the stylistic model he needed to express fully the theme he had discovered in New York. In a public library in Oslo, Bly learned about the European and South American surrealist tradition of modern poetry, an attractive countercurrent to the Anglo-American Eliotic tradition. Poets such as Georg Trakl of Austria, Pablo Neruda of Chile, and Juan Ramon Jiminez of Spain had a stunnning effect on Bly: "I felt avenues opening into kinds of imagination that I sort of dimly sensed somewhere off on the horizon, but I had never actually seen in English. . . . Wonderful imagery, exuberance, enthusiasm" (*T*, 49).

In retrospect it appears that Bly's Minnesota experience of social conformity and repression, coupled with his New York experience of the liberation through inwardness, had predisposed him to respond favorably to a poetry celebrating the spiritual importance of the dark, unconscious side of human personality. These poets were the models Bly had been looking for, the ones not only to teach him but, more importantly, to encourage him in his own poetic expression of the inward life. Time and again during the years to come Bly would cite them, especially Neruda, as spiritual as well as poetic mentors, and he would point to their achievement when he sought justification for his deviation from and attacks on the prevailing American tradition of Eliotic modernism. Thus they represented for Bly both a possible poetic style and a usable poetic tradition, and he depended greatly upon both.

The discovery of surrealism in Norway had two immediate effects on Bly. First, he changed his own style, abandoning the metrical verse of his Harvard and Iowa years, as well as the ironic wit that was its hallmark. Instead, he began to write poems that reached for something else than the expression of intellectual distance from and disaffection with the modern world. He began to explore consciously the means of expressing the unconscious life, and he began to develop for that purpose a poetics which throughout his career has proved more inventive and adaptive than that of any other contemporary American poet. Second, Bly decided that others should share his discovery. While traveling his inward road, Bly also took an outward road that so many other poets of the time were to take—he decided to edit and publish his own little magazine.

The *Fifties*

One has only to read the bold proclamations of those many independent little magazines begun in the fifties and sixties to realize that creating a magazine required an enormous commitment of energy and spirit. Yet the roll call of Bly's generation who made that commitment was long, and a testament to the felt need of the younger generation for a poetic revolution, a break with the past unprecedented in America since the twenties. Cid Corman and Robert Creeley's *Origin*, Robert Kelly's *Trobar*, Jerome Rothenberg's *Poems From the Floating World*, Charles Olson's *Black Mountain Review*, John Logan's *Choice*, and Paul Carroll's *Big Table* are just some of the important new outlets for poetry at the beginning of the sixties. But Bly's was to become perhaps the most important of all: "No literary history of the last twenty years would be complete without reference to Bly's magazine, *The Sixties*."[17] Bly's inspiration was the poetry of the new imagination he had discovered in Norway: "If it interested me that much, it would, must, interest some other young poets. . . . When my wife and I came back from Europe in 1958 we settled in an old farmhouse. With William Duffy as the other editor, we put out our first issue" (*T*, 49–50) of the *Fifties*. Thus began the period of Bly's career that saw the development of the fourth orientation point on the map of Bly's poetic imagination, the *Fifties*, a magazine of poetry and literary criticism (later renamed the *Sixties* and the *Seventies* to keep current with the decade). The creation and maintenance over three decades of one of America's most important literary magazines symbolized for Bly a commitment to activism as well as a deeper commitment to the exploration and expression of the new imagination which he had discovered in Norway. The *Fifties* came to symbolize Robert Bly's involvement with the world—at first, primarily that of literary politics, but later the wider world of American society and politics. The magazine represented Bly's working out of a problem most American writers and literature professors of the 1950s chose to evade as either insoluble or irrelevant, the problem of establishing a viable relationship between the conflicting worlds of art and politics.

From its beginning the *Fifties* took an aggressive stance against three elements of the literary establishment of its day. This triad included the editors of the important journals in the publishing system; those established, generally older poets who wrote a formal, abstract poetry—the antithesis of the associational, image-based free verse of the surrealist tradition; and finally, the New Critics, the dominant school of literary criticism in the 1950s, firmly entrenched in America's colleges and universities. In his very first issue Bly interviewed the editor of the *New York Times Book Review,* which was then, as it is today, "perhaps the most powerful reviewing medium in the country,"[18] and exposed him as a relatively untrained journalist-manager, rather than the knowledgeable literary critic the public imagined, whose reviews did not deserve the enormous weight they had in the success or failure of a writer's book or reputation. Further, the *Fifties* instituted two permanent features, "Madame Tussaud's Wax Museum," and the "Award of the Blue Toad," which satirized all aspects of this literary establishment. Bly awarded a Blue Toad to Gilbert Highet, editor of *Horizon,* who had attacked modern poetry in general and Ezra Pound in particular for not being understandable, simple, enough.[19] Another Blue Toad Award went to Norman Cousins, editor of the *Saturday Review,*[20] for putting out what Bly called a boring, stupid magazine. Bly cited for inclusion in Madame Tussaud's Wax Museum examples of stuffy, rhetorical poetry gathered from the work of the poet-editors of three of America's most influential periodicals: John Ciardi of the *Saturday Review,* Howard Moss of the *New Yorker,* and John Hollander of the *Partisan Review.*[21] Bly included also two academic poets: Yvor Winters, for writing a poetry so abstract as to be devoid of images,[22] and John Crowe Ransom, for writing falsely "poetic" poetry, weighted down with "inverted sentences, archaic usages, Sunday-afternoon meters and bashful language."[23] Finally, Bly attacked the prevailing standards of literary criticism as taught in American universities, especially their emphasis on form as the primary aspect of poetry, by awarding a Blue Toad Award to the commonly used textbook *Understanding Poetry.* Bly accused its authors, New Critics Robert Penn Warren and Cleanth Brooks, of an academic's bias favoring poetry that was understandable, that is, rational and capable of explication, rather than highly imaginative and associational. Because Brooks and Warren included eight poems by A. E. Housman while omitting Walt Whitman altogether, and because they completely ignored French, Spanish, German, or Chinese poets, their book "should have been called *Understanding A. E. Housman*."[24] All these and other such humorous jibes at the establishment were secondary to Bly's insightful criticism of his contemporary poets, and to the thoughtfulness of his essays on the traditions of modern poetry and their relevance to his generation.

From the first issue of Bly's magazine there had been intimations also of his willingness to mix political with literary criticism. For instance, the first issue of the *Fifties* ends with a full-page political joke, in the black humor mode of the day, about the healthful effects of atomic fallout and strontium-90, which were well-publicized products of atmospheric testing of nuclear weapons in the early sixties. The third issue attacks the coziness of religion and business in America in a section of social satire ironically titled "Ideas By Which We Live." An essay in issue 6 (1962) on the literary subject of the separation of form and content in art, titled "On the Necessary Aestheticism of Modern Poetry," provides Bly's most impressive statement of the necessary connection he felt existed between art and politics; it speaks to the essentially political issue of settling for a national poetry that refuses to address public issues, which is what the New Criticism advocated. Bly attacks the literary critic Ransom for praising modern American poets for avoiding moral issues, and also for his "elegant isolationism" that ignores the modern poetry of Europe and South America, which has a tradition of addressing political subjects. Bly then makes a proclamation, in early 1962, that foreshadows his poetry and criticism of the Vietnam period, and that expresses the sentiments of an entire generation of young American poets: "The greatness of modern poetry is that it is able to describe the sights and sounds of modern life, as well as the powerful ideas, such as self-interest, dictatorship, colonialism, and the political chaos that lies beneath it."[25] Such a statement was antithetical to the received beliefs of the American literary establishment of 1962, yet within five years it would describe very accurately the subject matter of a significant number of American poems. Robert Bly and his magazine had a leading role in this major revolution of sensibility in American literature.

In the first issue of the *Fifties* Robert Bly declared his allegiance to all poets "writing in what we have called, for want of a better word, the new imagination."[26] Bly announced that the two aims of his magazine were to publish the work of foreign poets who should be known to Americans, and to publish useful criticism for American poets. These two aims were more than fulfilled. In the first six issues, from 1958 through 1962, the magazine published translations of Gunnar Ekelof, Gottfried Benn, Juan Ramon Jiminez, Mirko Tuma, Antonio Machado, Lorca, no fewer than sixty pages of nineteenth- and twentieth-century French poetry, as well as Blas Otero, Paal Brekke, and Eugenio Montale. A collection of interviews with sixteen young American poets, conducted during 1960–61, includes many references to the European and Latin American poets who had been featured prominently in Bly's magazine. Indeed, one young American poet remarked that such writers as Lorca and Neruda were "becoming almost 'standard' poets now."[27] As recent critics have noted, it was "Bly's work as poet translator and editor" which made these Continental and Latin American surrealists the "principal" influences on the emerging American poetry of the sixties.[28] In these same issues Bly published essays under the pseudonym of "Crunk" on the work of such young, contemporary American poets as Robert Creeley, Donald Hall, W. S. Merwin, John Logan, and Gary Snyder. As Bly explained, "at that time the poets such as Creeley and Simpson were only thirty and thirty-two years old, but we published an essay on them as if they were seventy or eighty years old and tried to discuss what they had done so far in their work and tried to make criticisms that would be of real value to the poet himself" (*T*, 49).

The evolution of the "Crunk" essays (all but the one on Gary Snyder written by Bly) suggests much of the symbolic importance of the magazine for the poet himself, as well as provides an important record of Bly's ideas about poetry from 1958 onward. The first ten issues of the *Fifties* and the *Sixties* span the period from 1958 to 1968, and every issue but one (when Bly signs his own name to an aggressive attack on James Dickey) contains an essay by the Bly-persona Crunk. In general, the essays present Crunk praising or attacking other poets insofar as they follow the agenda of Bly's heralded new imagination; that is, insofar as they have a style broadly characterized as image-based, and relate their subjects somehow to the importance of the inward, unconscious life. These requirements of style and subject at times lead Bly into a "manifesto-criticism,"[29] with Crunk seeming to be engaged in a quasi-crusade. In the early years of the magazine this muscular criticism was limited to literary battles, with an occasional assault on those ever-popular bogeymen, "the middle class" and the

associated evils of materialism and conformity. But by the mid-1960s
the Crunk essays had changed from teaching poets about their craft
and about the possibilities of the new imagination to preaching
against poets for their politics rather than their poetry. This change
in the purpose and tone of the essays reflects larger changes, both in
Bly's own poetry and in his sense of the mission of a poet in the world
during a time of political crisis. The changes reflect also the ever-
deepening American involvement in the Vietnam War, and especially
the poet's growing involvement in the antiwar movement. An analysis of several representative Crunk essays from the early, middle, and
late periods (1959, 1964, 1967) will not only illustrate these
changes, but also suggest their significance for Bly's evolving definitions of poetry and of the acceptable parameters of a literary career.

Bly's Crunk essay on Donald Hall in the third issue of the *Fifties*[30]
provides a typical example of Bly's early building of specifically literary judgments on a base of sociopolitical and psychological critique.
Donald Hall is the third subject chosen by Crunk, after Louis Simpson and Robert Creeley. Hall is Bly's friend, former classmate, and
editorial colleague on the *Harvard Advocate*. As an assistant editor at
the *Paris Review*, Hall certainly must have been instrumental in providing Bly his most consistent and prestigious opportunity for publishing his poetry during the twelve years between Harvard and Bly's
first book. Yet the Crunk essay on Hall begins by declaring that
Hall's poetry always makes Crunk think of the middle class—certainly a lukewarm opening for a poetry review in 1959. Crunk proceeds to discuss the failure of American poets in general to establish
themselves as "independent from the middle class or any other class"
(32), unlike the poets of Ireland, France, Spain, or South America.
Crunk thinks Hall's work presents unrecognized characteristics of this
American struggle between the poet and the middle class, and Crunk
brings in terms from social and psychological criticism to describe
Hall's poems about "Father, God, and middle class society" (39),
even seeing Hall's use of regular iambic meter as evidence of a subconscious desire to appease "the cultural father" of the American middle class, the English. Crunk declares that Hall's poetry evinces the
same "mingled longing and loathing" (39) that Freud predicted for
any son's struggle with a father. The key for Crunk to the poet's win-
ning this struggle with the middle class is not to write about their
failings, as so many contemporary poets have (both academic poets
and those of the Beat school are cited), but to involve one's self in the

continuing struggle for what the middle class can never understand, "a secret life. . . . an inner life" (46). The explorer of the inner life is the central image of the poet "as developed by Yeats, and the Spanish, and this image seems the one least developed in America" (46). Crunk concludes his attention to Hall's poetry by praising his more recent poems, citing in them evidence that Hall "is capable of development and of movement" (44). And he saves his harshest words for others, including reviewers of Hall's work, who oppose the poetry of the new imagination, the poetry of the "inner life," by labeling it dangerous "experimentation" (46). Thus Crunk-Bly has brought the discussion round from the poetry of Hall to the poetry of the new imagination—whose subject is precisely the inner life, whose style is free verse and other forms of dangerous experimentation. He has written the sort of essay about a poet that Auden practiced in the 1950s in his widely praised introductions to the annual winners of the Yale Younger Poets series—discussion of the poet, but of another, larger subject as well, one occasioned by the poet's work. Here Crunk has suggested correspondences between poetic, sociopolitical, and psychological attitudes; but he has kept in focus always the central subject, the poetry of Hall and of the new imagination.

Bly's two essays on James Dickey (1964, 1967) illustrate not only the general tenor of the criticism in the *Sixties* but also the increasing symbolic significance for Bly of publishing a magazine, of having a public voice which gives the poet-editor a public role. If the role of champion of new and unknown poets is the benevolent face of a poet-editor of an influential literary magazine, then the role of political partisan and ad hominem critic must be the dangerous face that can vitiate his literary judgments. In the winter 1964 issue Bly as Crunk wrote and published a favorable critique, "The Work of James Dickey."[31] He admired the theme of evolutionary transformation that he found in the Southerner's poetry, the "spiritual struggle . . . the struggle of an animal to become man" (41). Crunk also approved of Dickey's drive for the infinite, his pushing "to the very edges of his perception" (55), and he praised Dickey as a fantasist with a "staggering gift for the image" (55), the psychologically true image of the surrealist rather than the word picture of the "dreary realist." These characteristics of Dickey's subject matter and style are ones Bly had applauded in many other poets—they are all typical of the Spanish surrealists, for instance, as well as of Bly's own work.

Yet in this first essay on Dickey Crunk notes also certain limitations, and these literary lapses are nearly all described as though they were personal, ethical lapses of Dickey the man. For instance, Crunk qualifies his admiration of Dickey's "sudden passages from the bestial to the angelic" by wondering about the missing "human battleground between," what Crunk calls "the slow struggle to improve character" (50) that is necessary to support such sudden leaping. Crunk also dislikes certain aspects of Dickey's style, again criticizing it in psychological terms, attacking the poet's "dactyllic power-mad rhythm" (51) as well as his excessive use of "me" and "my," which for Bly creates a "curious narcissism in the poem" (52). But overall, Dickey's poetry of nature-consciousness and surrealistic leaping received high praise from Bly in 1964.

Two years later, in the spring 1967 issue, Bly published a second essay on the poet, "The Collapse of James Dickey,"[32] which reveals much more about the danger of psychic inflation inherent in publishing one's own magazine than it does about the nature of Dickey's poetry. Significantly, the essay is signed by Bly himself, not Crunk. This switch from persona to real name symbolizes the transformation that Bly's editorial voice underwent—the effort toward objectivity and disinterestedness is abandoned completely, as the editor-persona is supplanted by the political partisan. A similar metamorphosis was occurring in Bly's poetry too, as it evolved from ironic to bitterly satiric in its treatment of America's prowar contingent in *The Light around the Body*. During the two years between the essays, the Vietnam war had changed dramatically, radically polarizing public opinion on the question of American involvement. Bly had crisscrossed the country as co-chairman of the American Writers Against the Vietnam War, leading antiwar "read-ins" on college campuses. Bly's intensity of feeling mirrored that of the majority of the American people (both sides, whether for or against the war, were beyond the point of tolerating the opposition). But while Bly's emotionalism was not unusual for the times, its intensity colors his statements about Dickey in ways that undercut his argument. The tone of the criticism is obviously occasioned by something other than Dickey's poetry—it has spilled over into Bly's literary criticism from his greatly increased public role in the larger national debate over the war.

Reviewing Dickey's book *Buckdancer's Choice*, Bly immediately attacks both author and work: "The subject of the poems is power, and the tone of the book is gloating—a gloating about power over others" (70). Bly argues that Dickey has written three long poems about subjects that should evoke moral outrage—slavery, firebombing, and peeping toms—but instead Dickey is fascinated by these subjects and has written three poems implicitly celebrating the fantasies of power that are the psychological cause of such acts. The poem "Slave Quarters," according to Bly, "pretends to be a poem about the moral issue of ownership, but lingers in the fantasies of ownership." Bly calls it "one of the most repulsive poems ever written in American literature" (71). He attacks not only the poem's content, but also its tone and language. It has a "smugness beyond race prejudice" that is convinced that "Negroes are objects" (72); and since a poem's language "can be no better than the quality of the imagination" of the poet, not only the poem but Dickey as well are "dead and without feeling" (72). Bly here is measuring the language against the subject and feeling that he thinks ought to be, but isn't, there—the "masculine and adult sorrow" (70) about social injustice; Dickey, of course, intended his language to express a different subject and evoke different feelings. Bly criticizes the poem "Firebombing" in a similar vein, blaming its serious flaws on an immoral sociopolitical attitude toward its subject: "in its easy acceptance of brutality, the poem is deeply middle class" (75). And to correspond to Dickey's admiration for racist power in "Slave Quarter," and his acceptance of unjust sociopolitical power in "Firebombing," Bly discovers in "The Fiend"—about peeping toms—Dickey's hidden fascination with psychological power, that of the "utterly cold" person over the one who feels "human warmth and enthusiasm," like the power "the Snow Queen has over the human children" (75).

This interrelationship that Bly assumes must exist between a person's attitudes toward racism and his attitudes toward other manifestations of unjust power in the personal and political realms was expressed in a feminist-inspired slogan popular during that time, "the personal is the political." A corollary of that belief is that there is a natural, inevitable, perhaps subconscious but often easily discernible unity between a person's life and work. Bly's essay takes up this theme by noting that while other critics have praised Dickey's poems, they did so on the false assumption that the poems were not about Dickey, but about one of his consciously created and aesthetically distanced literary personas, a mask supposedly separate from the author's face. Bly denies this possibility, claiming that the poems in their "psychic blurriness" reveal Dickey's "naked longing for power" (77). The book's "sensationalism" of subject matter betrays the author's true sentiments, which Bly and others[33] find not only aesthetically displeasing but also morally offensive.

Bly has always disapproved of the modernistic poetic strategy of using such a persona-mask to distance an author from his poem. But here he raises a different issue, for he cites the blurriness of Dickey's poetic focus as evidence that he was evading the moral issues of the subject matter because he secretly harbored immoral desires for power. The implicit ad hominem nature of this argument is made explicit as Bly's essay proceeds. He argues for a necessary "unity of the man and his work" (78), and thus tries to justify using knowledge of the author's life not only to attack his poetry but also to impute hidden motives to it. Bly notes that James Dickey is in favor of the Vietnam War, and that he also has bragged about making lots of money from his poetry, and Bly suggests that perhaps these aspects of Dickey's life are "associated somehow with the abrupt decline in the quality of his work" (79). Bly's attack rises to a concluding crescendo when he declares that Dickey at age forty-three has become "a huge blubbering poet, . . . a toady to government. . . . a sort of Georgia Cracker Kipling" (79) in his support of the new American Empire. Criticism of this sort draws more attention to the critic than to the object of his wrath; it vividly demonstrates the force upon Bly's sensibility of the external pressure generated by the Vietnam War, and probably even more by the sudden and intense public role he assumed by becoming co-chairman of the American Writers Against the Vietnam War, as well as by championing through his magazine a new poetry which from the beginning was entangled with a vague but for Bly powerful vision of a new morality. Nevertheless, in its assumptions about the relation of the poet to his work, and the work to the audience, this essay is an important document of the dominant public sensibility of the sixties. Unfortunately, it illustrates also the extent to which both ethical crusades (Bly's) and the false equation of the sensationalistic grotesque with profound experience (Dickey's) threatened and sometimes distorted the aesthetic judgments of that generation. Still, it is a measure of Bly's centrality to his times that even in the poet's failures a truth about his generation is revealed.

The *Fifties,* then, is Bly's testimony to his belief in the importance of inwardness, and especially of its expression in poetry, for the public world. His magazine is motivated not only by the usual literary impulses that give rise to literary magazines, but also by Bly's strong moral impulse to improve and perfect the public world. This mixture of the literary and moral, while not uncommon in American literary criticism (the conservative moral bias of Eliot and the New Critics is not irrelevant to the pseudo-scientific objectivism of such tenets as the affective fallacy and the intentional fallacy), can be easily overlooked or misunderstood by those who fail to recognize the source of the passion. Bly's attacks in the *Fifties* on the literary and political establishment, and the polemical editorial attitude that provides an important and ongoing subtext for every feature of the magazine, both originate in the poet's strong belief in the universal truth of the major theme expressed in his poetry of the new imagination, the necessity of man's traveling the inward road.

Chapter Two

The Poetics of the New Imagination: *Silence in the Snowy Fields*

While he was writing for and editing the *Fifties,* Bly was publishing his own poetry elsewhere, both in journals and anthologies. But in 1962 his career as an important new American poet properly begins, with the publication of two books. The first, *The Lion's Tail and Eyes: Poems Written Out of Laziness and Silence,*[1] was a joint collection of poems by Bly, James Wright, and William Duffy. The second was Bly's first book, *Silence in the Snowy Fields,*[2] published by Wesleyan University Press in what was then considered "the most distinguished American poetry series."[3] The books were well received by the critics, and taken together they stand as a statement and illustration of the new kind of imagination that Bly had championed in the *Fifties,* the kind of poetry that he was to develop through the rest of his career.

Most contemporary reviewers praised *Silence.* They categorized Bly's poetry as pastoral and/or transcendental, observing that the subject matter was frequently either the countryside of Minnesota or else what appeared to be the poet's vaguely spiritual aspirations. But in retrospect it is clear that the enduring basis of Bly's work has always been the psychological theme of man's inward life and the act of perception/discovery necessary to connect with and develop it. In his prefacing note to *The Lion's Tail and Eyes* Bly had emphasized that content, not form, was his intended subject. Yet he went on to identify his content as organic form personified. His stated poetic subject was the inherent relationship between one's inner self and his outer actions, a relationship Bly believed to be as organic and natural as that between a man and his "ear, or a hand."[4] The book's title emphasized Bly's enduring concern for the psychological theme of evolutionary human nature and its attendant transformations. The "Lion" of the title is identified as a poem expressive of the unconscious part of the psyche, which can reveal itself only if properly captured by the poet and espied by the reader precisely at the moment when the beast "is changing from his old ancient substance back into a visible body."[5] Man's collective, evolutionary past is the repository of this "ancient substance"; and unlike a poetry based on the image-as-picture, where the lion stands still for all to see, Bly's poetry strives for the dynamic image that can express the moment of transformation which magically leads both poet and reader back to the "inward world."[6] Thus, the poems in this book attempt to limn this ancient legacy of a collective archetypal past by capturing hints of it, by tracing only the evanescent lion's "tail and eyes" as it moves in and out of our consciousness. Such inward psychic dynamism and energy can exist completely apart from outward physical action, as the passive states of "Laziness and Silence" invoked in the book's title make clear. This contrast between inward dynamism and outward silence and calm is also a prevalent theme of Bly's *Silence,* which includes half of the poems published earlier in *The Lion's Tail and Eyes.*

Bly's first book, *Silence,* was a selection and arrangement of work done over a period of some nine years. Bly used the title and the epigraph to unite the whole work both imagistically and thematically, and he grouped the forty-four poems into three sections: "Eleven Poems of Solitude," "Awakening," and "Silence on the Roads." Within each section there is a loose affinity among the poems by subject matter and direction. The author intends a development from section to section, as suggested by the section titles, a development of the poet's awareness of his task: first, meditation in solitude, then "awakening," and finally commitment to the poet's vocation of following the inward road of self-exploration. Further evidence of Bly's intention that the book stand as a whole, with an overall development beyond its individual poems, is provided by the significant changes he made several years later[7] for the British edition of *Silence.* Also, within each section the last poem seems to answer the first, to round out a natural development from an earlier stage to an ever-increasing reliance on the unconscious sources in the poet's own psyche. Finally, the imagery of silence, snow, and darkness pervades the poetry and helps unify the book. Still, there remains a "selected poems" quality about *Silence* that is absent in Bly's later books (with the exception of *Loving a Woman in Two Worlds*). For instance, the poet intersperses several of his early sonnets, a prose poem, and even an imitation of

Wallace Stevens within a book whose predominant form is the free-verse poem of three stanzas.

Silence in the Snowy Fields, whether viewed as a collection of poetry unto itself or as the first major work in the continuum of Robert Bly's career, provides an introduction to three crucial aspects of the poetics of what Bly liked to call "the new imagination."[8] The first is the aesthetic experience of reading Bly's poetry—of experiencing his style of consciousness. From the book's first poem it is immediately obvious that Bly confronts the reader with a poetry that intends to convey an experience of another's consciousness, one extending beyond the limits of rational intellect. How Bly writes this experience, and whether he is successful in his intent, remains a subject of lively critical debate, not only from poem to poem but also from book to book throughout Bly's career.

The second topic of major importance is Bly's concept of the image and the process of image-making. The image is the keystone of Bly's poetics, for it joins his belief that poetry should be an expression of man's twofold consciousness with his search for the formal properties of a poem which can enable poetry to express that magical moment when the unconscious reveals itself to the conscious, when the Lion becomes visible. Indeed, Bly's special concept of the deep image is more important to Bly's poetics than any single theme he writes about, for the success of this image in allowing the poet's unconscious to connect with the reader's unconscious must be the strongest evidence to prove the truth of Bly's major theme, that there is in fact an essential correspondence and unity between all men as well as between man and nature because of the continuing viability of their shared evolutionary, unconscious past. When Bly's images succeed, the reader is convinced of the possibility of such a connection; indeed, the reader acknowledges his own twofold consciousness by assenting to the effectiveness, the aesthetic truth, of Bly's deep image. Thus the experience of reading Bly the way he hopes to be read depends greatly on the validity of his special concept of the image. Similarly, Bly's concept of the image dictates his choice of poetic forms; Bly uses a fluid, emergent form—ranging from free verse to the prose poem—in order to support the image. Bly's outward poetic form, especially his line, appears flabby and even prosaic unless it is seen as appropriate to a poetry whose inner energy is based on the generative rhythm of image-building and perception-making.

The third and final aspect of Bly's poetics is the meaning and role of the major themes he introduces in this first book, themes which in varied form endure throughout his work. A crucial corollary question involves the relationship between theme and image in Bly's work, and to what degree they mutually reinforce each other. Bly's major themes are two: an elucidation of human nature as twofold, consisting of both the conscious and the unconscious, and an exploration of the myriad correspondences between man's nature as a creature of twofold consciousness and Nature herself, including Nature's other creatures. But the role of themes in Bly's work, and of interpretation, argument, and analysis, is often secondary to the poetic reenactment of a process of perception/discovery which these poems mean to convey. Thus the reader of Bly is asked to respond first and foremost to an experience, not to analyze it by thematic interpretation. The process of a Bly poem is primary, especially in *Silence,* for through that emergent event the enduring theme of the discovery of the inward man is made visible.

The Reading Experience

The experience of reading *Silence* is one of reading about and, more importantly, sharing in the sense of freedom that comes from participation in what Bly's erstwhile mentor,[9] the neo-Jungian James Hillman, terms "soul-making.[10] Bly's poetry is engaged in an unceasing effort to build harmony between the conscious and unconscious parts of the human personality, to achieve what Jung's disciple Erich Neumann defined as "psychic wholeness, in which the consciousness of every human being is creatively allied with the content of the unconscious."[11] Reading Bly is not limited to experiencing the revelations of the shifting nature of perception and consciousness, revelations whose emotional dynamism and magnitude in the poems of *Silence* are much greater than would seem warranted by such minor perceptual shifts as snow covering cornfields, or lights going on at evening in a very ordinary landscape. Rather, Bly asks the reader to experience also the emotion of purposefulness, and even providence, which can accompany such creative alignments of the inner man and the outer world, the emotions of psychic discovery and creation. Bly's poetry is not intended to describe a physical world. Bly's Minnesota of snow, darkness, lakes, barns, and trees is ordinary, and perhaps tedious, only if the reader fails to heed Bly's epigraph to *Silence,* the mystic

Jacob Boehme's dictum "We are all asleep in the outward man," and thus fails to recognize the poem's display of the psychodynamics of the emergent inner man, which is the true subject of the poetry.

The Jungian concept of a collective unconscious memory, formed from common experiences imprinted during life's evolution and passed on to each newborn human being, plays an important role in *Silence.* Bly's first book, unlike later ones, does not ask the reader to be familiar with either the terminology or the ramifications for society and politics of the collective unconscious. But one must recognize the uses Bly makes of this concept in trying to evoke the common human experience that the origins of thought and action seem deeper and darker than rationalism usually acknowledges. Certainly such a concept is well suited to a poetry devoted to exploring man's symbol-making impulses, to expressing those salutary, late-night "thoughts full of dreams" (58).

Bly addresses directly the subject of the collective unconscious in "Surprised by Evening." He begins the poem by invoking the presence of an obscure but strongly felt collective past, declaring in the voice some have criticized as "bardic"[12] that "There is unknown dust that is near us" (15). Bly links this presence with the coming of evening's darkness, which, surprisingly enough to creatures like rational men who think themselves "born for the daylight," brings with it a different kind of vision and wisdom, a state of nonrational consciousness in which "our skin shall see far off, as it does under water." Under the water's surface, beneath the awareness threshold of the conscious mind, is "a net drawn down with dark fish," primordial creatures of the unconscious spawned in our evolutionary past, obscure yet deeply felt, that influence and even sustain the conscious, "daylight" life. To perceive/discover this strength in the unconscious parts of the human psyche is to learn to welcome the coming of evening, the gradual, refreshing, welling-up of "the quiet waters of the night."

In *Silence,* and throughout Bly's career, this crucial discovery of the salutary power of the collective unconscious is imaged as the discovery of a treasure. He calls it the "true/ gift, beneath the pale lakes of Minnesota" (*Si*, 56) in what may be the book's best known poem, "After Drinking All Night with a Friend, We Go Out in a Boat at Dawn to See Who Can Write the Best Poem." The invocation of mysterious depths and profound presences which this collective unconscious/submerged treasure motif projects is intended to disarm the reader's critical faculty and encourage a meditative receptivity (not unlike that felt after drinking all night). Bly's appeal to elements of the fantastic, such as buried treasures and powerful "unknown dust," is so directly counter to the reader's ordinary habits of understanding and interpreting primarily with the conscious intellect that Bly's poetry has always been an acquired taste. In *Silence* Bly is not always successful in achieving a poetic tone that suggests presence without seeming pretentiously bardic, purposelessly obscure, or both. But a reading of the complete book not only familiarizes the reader with Bly's strategy of appealing directly to the unconscious, but also convinces him of Bly's serious intent in using such an approach. In the poetry of *Silence* Bly is trying to do what he once praised in the great Chilean poet Neruda—to move under the surface of things, trying to know "everything from the bottom up (which is the right way to learn the nature of a thing)."[13]

The experience of reading Bly is influenced not only by the poet's choice of subject, such as the collective unconscious, but also stylistic choices. It is important to recognize *Silence* as a thorough rejection of the predominant poetic style of 1962, a style often ingeniously rhetorical in language, extremely egotistic in voice and tone, and in its choice of subject matter given to a self-revelation which in its sensationalism comes perilously close to self-exploitation. Bly attacked the poetry of Robert Lowell, whom he had once emulated. Bly cited Lowell's failure, especially in *Life Studies,* to write about anything but ego-oriented human life, ignoring not only the world of nature but also of people in other countries. Bly disliked the sensationalism of these so-called "confessional" poets as symptomatic of their failure to write "a poetry that goes deep into the human being, much deeper than the ego, and at the same time is aware of many other beings."[14]

Instead of the anguished "I" of the confessional poets, spoken from behind a persona-mask, Bly's poetry in *Silence* is spoken by an "I" who is virtually identical with the poet himself. Bly often attacked the intellectual style that used a persona to achieve an ironic distance between a poet and his voice, and even accused poets of evading moral responsibility by hiding behind a persona. Bly argued that the persona technique made poetic language a separate, privileged language, and kept the reader so distanced from the poem that he could never discover himself within it nor feel truly moved by it. Bly places great weight on the ability of a poet's voice to estabish a close relationship with the reader, and he has said that achieving this tone is the goal of his method of composition. For instance, Bly claims that he never revises a line in the usual sense of the term—by substituting a new word, image, or idea—but instead writes a completely new line if the first one does not have the right tone. The "I" of *Silence* does not address itself to the usual concerns of the anxious intellect, but rather invites the reader to enter into a musing, reflective, and even meditative mood. In *Silence* Bly's voice is relatively passive, certainly not ego-assertive, so that words and images remain associated with a personal voice, yet retain much of the freedom and authority associated with an omniscient third-person narrator. The reader never senses that the speaker is a character writing his own life study.

"Three Kinds of Pleasures," the first poem of *Silence,* illustrates how simple language and, especially, an unobtrusive speaking "I" are central to Bly's poetics:

I

Sometimes, riding in a car, in Wisconsin
Or Illinois, you notice those dark telephone poles
One by one lift themselves out of the fence line
And slowly leap on the gray sky—
And past them, the snowy fields.

II

The darkness drifts down like snow on the picked cornfields
In Wisconsin: and on these black trees
Scattered, one by one,
Through the winter fields—
We see stiff weeds and brownish stubble,
And white snow left now only in the wheel tracks of the
    combine.

III

It is a pleasure, also, to be driving
Toward Chicago, near dark,
And see the lights in the barns.
The bare trees more dignified than ever,
Like a fierce man on his deathbed,
And the ditches along the road half full of a private snow.

"Three Kinds of Pleasures" is typical of Bly's early poems of the new imagination. It is a poem about the act of perception, apart from the significance of the thing perceived, as a form of psychic discovery; in this it is similar to many other poems in *Silence,* such as "Getting Up Early," "After Working," or "Snowfall in the Afternoon." It has three parts, so marked, and a first-person speaker engaged in the ordinary act of driving his car through the snow-covered farm country of the flat Midwest as evening falls. What, the reader asks, can provide "three kinds of pleasure" in such a barren scene? Bly does not offer the pleasure of the ironic mind celebrating its own creative power by creating elaborate conceits from observing an ordinary object. Nor does Bly speak out of a confessional anguish, seeing in the very barrenness of the landscape a metaphor for the bleakness of his own soul. Bly eschews these approaches, so common among the poets of 1962. Instead, Bly writes a poem having the simplicity of a Zen meditation, in which as the perception changes and grows, so does the perceiver. Bly's poem has a speaker in simple language recording with minimal comment these pleasurable perceptual shifts: telephone poles "slowly leap" (*Si,* 18) on the sky (as he drives closer, they loom larger), darkness "drifts down like snow," lights go on as evening gives way to darkness, while bare trees grow darker and "more dignified than ever." The speaker enjoys both the subtle changes in the scene as well as his own developing consciousness of it. He meanders via car (like the drifting boat of "After Drinking All Night"), passing through the changing rhythms of riding and driving, through the shifting visual landscape observed under the different weather conditions of light and dark and snow. In perceiving this landscape, the poet-speaker meditatively interacts with it as well, and even begins to re-figure and re-create it in his own imagination. But the plot of this poem is the growth of the perceiving poet toward a relationship with the landscape he observes, a growth from passive observation to creative personification and simile in the last stanza, building toward the symbol of fields of "private snow," whose symbolic significance is generated by the poet's discovery of a corresponding resonance within his own psyche.

In *Silence* the reader is spoken to by an "I" who is never ego-assertive, subordinating what he sees to his own attitudes about it. Rather, Bly respects the act of perception as a road to the discovery of truth in both the outer and inward worlds. For Bly the true poet is the one "who sees in human beings a part of the universe, for whom human nature is interesting not because it is human, but because it is nature."[15] Further, Bly implicitly assumes that observation

will lead to subtle interaction, mutual recognition of man and nature's shared evolutionary heritage. In this meditative mood Bly is
able to allow images to grow into symbols, to accumulate associations
and thereby symbolic significance within a particular poem. For instance, in "Three Kinds of Pleasures" the significance of the "snowy
fields" of stanza 1 grows to become the poet's symbolic vision, looking both outward and inward, of a "private snow" of stanza 3; and
the broadest significance of the "snowy fields" of the book's title
grows from all the associations and developments built upon that image throughout the whole book, and even into later books. Similarly,
the "silence" invoked in this first poem, as well as in the titles of
Bly's first two books, underscores the strengths of his plain poetics—
without the noise of ironic flourish or confessional anguish. But Bly's
silence also symbolizes the strong, supportive presence of the energy
of the unconscious, which lies dormant beneath those snowy fields
which to a rationalist's eye, trained for scanning surface movement,
might seem to cover nothing. Thus the book's title is indeed appropriate, for the experience of reading Bly's *Silence* poems is intended to
be one of growing attuned to the sound of the deepening silence that
accompanies the revelations of the inner man, here expressed in a simple language by an aware but nonegoistic speaker.

Robert Bly's Image

The importance of the image to Bly's poetry cannot be overstated.
Various terms have been used to describe his work: *surrealist, deep image, emotive,* and *radical presence.* But all share a common focus on the
image (not line, rhythm, or theme) as the most prominent stylistic
event of Bly's poetry. Robert Kelly, originator of the oft-used term
"deep image,"[16] insisted in 1962, as did Bly himself, on the distinction between the image as a picture of external reality and the image
as an expression of inner reality. Kelly declared that "the Poetry of
Images (stress on Poetry: it's not a technique) is essentially a mode of
Vision."[17] Kelly disliked the term surrealism; he argued that, while
it might accurately describe the initial stage that the deep image poet
goes through, the final product of surrealist poets like Breton is very
different from that of the new poetry of deep image. Bly himself
made a similar distinction between false and true surrealism. He attacked poetry that attempted merely to break down the structure of
the conscious mind, pursuing the goal of derangement characteristic
of the French tradition of Baudelaire and Rimbaud. Bly contrasted

this goal with that of the so-called new surrealism, as practiced by poets of the new imagination such as James Wright, Neruda, and himself, poets who disregard the conscious, intellectual structure of the mind entirely and, "by the use of images, try to bring forward another reality from *inward* experience."[18] Similarly, Jerome Rothenberg explained the intention of this new kind of deep image poetry as "an exploration of the unconscious region of the mind in such a way that the unconscious [of the poet] is speaking to the unconscious [of the reader]."[19] As one critic acknowledged in 1962, "Rothenberg, Kelly and Bly are considered, personally and by way of their magazines, the leading agitators for a poetry based on 'Image.' "[20]

Two helpful analyses of Bly's image, examining especially the two very different poetic goals inherent in using the image as inward reality rather than as a picture of external reality, have been presented in two studies of Bly and other poets of the sixties. The first book uses the term "the emotive imagination"[21] to characterize the common ground held by Bly, James Wright, Louis Simpson, and William Stafford, important young poets of the sixties. This study argues that the goal of these poets was "understanding through feeling,"[22] and was consciously opposed to the understanding through rational explication that the New Critics had asserted should be the goal of all great poetry. This book's argument is blurred somewhat by the authors' insistence that early twentieth-century imagism is an illuminating antecedent of the deep-image poetry of the sixties. Bly has on several occasions vigorously denied imagism a place in the deep-image tradition. He wanted the break with the modernist's goal of intellectualizing the world to be much more radical: "An image and a picture differ in that the image, being the natural speech of the imagination, cannot be drawn from or inserted back into the real world."[23]

A second important book on Bly and the poets of the sixties employs the term "radical presence"[24] to characterize both the poetic style and goal of those poets. The critic Charles Altieri, like Kelly and Rothenberg, shows that Bly's particular form of presence is consciously antagonistic to intellectual understanding, for it insists on "the imaginative act as a denial of the ego" (83) hence a denial of the rational, of ego-understanding, and it also insists on the image "not as artifact, but as a specific way of seeing or of participating in experience" (84). Altieri's thesis is that this goal commits the poets of the sixties, including Bly, to an "immanentist mode" of writing, responding to the new challenge "to imagine non-Christian sources of immanent value" (79), rather than the "symbolist mode" typical of their modern predecessors. In Bly's postmodern poetics the image must serve the ontological function of putting man in touch with the deepest, nonsubjective levels of his being; and it may, through that ontological discovery of self, serve both a social and a moral function, of helping the individual "combat the egocentric violence of American life" (85).

Bly himself uses the term *image* to include the widest range of imaginative expression of inner reality—from fundamental description of physical reality, through metaphor and parable, to symbol, archetype, and myth. Bly describes his image as an energy-generating event, by which the psyche "instead of depending on the outer world for support . . . begins somehow to create a third world, neither 'physical' nor 'inner' " (*T*, 259). However, Bly always tries to build his psychic image upon a physical base, even an image which might seem to be purely archetypal: "I agree an image can be 'close' to an archetype, but the way to ruin a poem is to put in a lot of archetypes. I insist the image is a physical thing" (*T*, 260). But within each poem in *Silence* a formal pattern of development, from descriptive image to symbol, occurs again and again. This pattern is intended to be expressive of the way the psyche mediates between the external world and its own inner world of personal and collective unconsciousness.

Thus Bly's poems intend to convey a sense of energy and activity in spite of their outwardly passive speaker and ordinary real-world subject matter of snow and farms. Indeed, a Bly poem is, taken by itself, one complete image, one emblem of the ongoing psychic process which is continually building images. Each poem-image is an emblem of Neumann's sought for harmony between conscious and unconscious mind, an emblem of Hillman's soul-making process. It is not a process that obeys the rational laws of logic, of syllogism and noncontradiction; nor does this psychic process limit itself to the pattern of faithful recording of the object observed that results in well-wrought pictures of the physical world. But it becomes familiar as one learns the poems. So that after reading *Silence,* one feels that the soul-making process implicit in Bly's image-building is itself the true subject of the poems, the ultimate theme and goal behind all of Bly's poetic acts.

Silence offers examples on many levels of the centrality of the image and image-building to Bly's poetics. The tripartite structure of many of the poems, and indeed of Bly's arranging of the book into three parts, corresponds to, and reinforces, his recurring pattern of building images into symbols. Often the three-part poem proceeds dialectically, with the collision of parts 1 and 2 generating part 3's synthesis, resolving and symbolizing the conflicts of parts 1 and 2. The earlier discussion of "Three Kinds of Pleasures" showed how Bly developed within a poem the image of snow into his own, symbolic "private snow." But Bly's image of snow develops across the poems as well, and even carries over ino Bly's second book; there, the crucial image of "the snowy field of the insane asylum" in "Sleet Storm on the Merritt Parkway" provides an especially good example of how Bly imbues images with resonances from book to book. Further, in interviews Bly has said that he still writes five or six "snowy fields" poems a year, which all add to the overall significance of this lifelong, fundamental symbol. Major images that Bly builds into symbols include darkness, water, solitude, waking, sleeping, and home.

"Snowfall in the Afternoon," the final poem of *Silence,* clearly illustrates Bly's symbol-building; it uses images that have appeared often in the first forty-three poems, yet redevelops them within the individual poetic context:

I

The grass is half-covered with snow.
It was the sort of snowfall that starts in late afternoon,
And now the little houses of the grass are growing dark.

II

If I reached my hands down, near the earth,
I could take handfuls of darkness!
A darkness was always there, which we never noticed.

III

As the snow grows heavier, the cornstalks fade farther away,
And the barn moves nearer to the house.
The barn moves all alone in the growing storm.

IV

The barn is full of corn, and moving toward us now,
Like a hulk blown toward us in a storm at sea;
All the sailors on deck have been blind for many years.

"Snowfall in the Afternoon" uses Bly's staples of snow, darkness, and barns to express in fresh ways the relationship between the inner and the outward man. More importantly, this last poem draws on meanings generated from the complex developed around these images throughout the book. Indeed, in this final poem Bly skillfully merges his two major images, snow and darkness, and grants them full symbolic powers. Bly presents a scene in which, because of the decreasing light of the crepuscule combined with an increasingly heavy snowstorm, the nature of the speaker's perception shifts radically, until his imaginative/symbolic vision completely replaces his literal, observing eyesight. The poet artfully presents these shifts of vision, so that the reader feels he is reenacting the experience of transition and transformation as he reads, thus experiencing as well as understanding the meaning of the poem. Bly renders this experience of perceptual development primarily through his symbol-building process.

The poem's first two stanzas act as one, for they describe the setting and link the snow and darkness visually and symbolically. The poet declares he could reach down into the snow and "take handfuls of darkness" (*Si*, 60), of the snow-darkness symbolic of the unconscious regions of the psyche with which the poet, reader, and book itself have by now become familiar: "A darkness was always there, which we never noticed." Stanza 3 continues the snow-darkness vision which, as in a dream, distorts reality for surreal, symbolic effects: the "cornstalks fade farther away, / And the barn moves nearer to the house." The barn may recall the image in the first poem of the book, the "lights in the barns" (*Si*, 11); indeed, this concluding poem recalls the beginning poem in tone and image, though now Bly is more overtly symbolic in his expression of the emergence of the unconscious, inward man. The movement of the barn toward the house answers the situation addressed in the preceding poem, expressed in the line "Something homeless is looking on the long roads"; here the approach of the barn toward the home signifies the increasing closeness of unconsciousness to consciousness in the poet's personality, of the place where the poet stores food for the winter and the place where he lives. The last stanza affirms this new alignment, for the barn is "full of corn, and moving toward us now," freighted with the inward and nourishing food that one can see only when the outward and snow-covered cornstalks have faded from sight. Here the barn is specifically associated with Bly's frequently used ship image, which has grown increasingly important in this final part of the book in comparing personality development, soul-making, to a voyage into the unconscious. The sailors on this ship, Bly says in his final poem, "have been blind for many years"; but literal sight isn't necessary to perceive the life of the unconscious. Rather, one needs the ability to discover and accept symbols from the unconscious, to become attuned as the poet does throughout this first book of poems to the sound of "silence in the snowy fields."

Robert Bly's Themes

The overarching theme of Robert Bly's career is what Jung called the "circumambulation of the self,"[25] the continual shuttling movement from unconscious to conscious, from darkness to light, which is the most important action in the development and individuation of a person's psyche, of his soul. Jung saw this movement to develop the inward life as the necessary destiny of the awakened person, the farthest reach of human wisdom, and Bly agrees. Bly's lesser themes, even though they may seem dominant in a particular book, must nevertheless all be considered finally as subservient to the poet's central task of elucidating this grand theme of soul-making. In *Silence* the presence of Jungian psychology is much less obvious than it is in the books to come, especially at the level of poetic theme. But it still remains an important influence, and occasionally a subtext, which informs the fullest appreciation and understanding of most of the poems. Bly's answers have been confusing on the question of his indebtedness to evolutionary depth psychology. He has said that he began reading Jung in 1961, though not "seriously"[26] until 1970. Nevertheless, anyone familiar with the concerns and terms of evolutionary depth psychology, from Bachofen through Jung, Erich Neumann, and James Hillman, will recognize that the thrust of Bly's poetry even in the first book is toward an exploration of the twofold nature of man, inward and outward, unconscious and conscious. Indeed, Bly's whole emphasis on image-building is based on the Jungian paradigm of personality development, on Jung's assumption of a continual interaction between the conscious ego and the personal and collective unconscious.

This psychic movement between unconscious and conscious is not to be confused with a desire for transcendence, for escape from the material world, although Bly's practice of building up associations around a central physical image may seem initially to suggest a transcendental urge. But in fact Bly's overarching theme of soul-making is inherently inconsistent with any desire for escape from this material world. Several associated themes, which became prominent at various points in Bly's career and are found in varying degrees in *Silence,* also emphasize the inward quest of Bly's poetry. These themes are Bly's belief in a continuing process of self-knowledge through self-discovery; his willing immersion in the historical and archetypal past, because of his belief in its formative influence on the present; and, finally, the poet's obvious love of and fine eye for the immediate details of the world of nature, of Minnesota weather, trees, and animals.

The first theme, the quest for self-discovery through the pursuit of an inward road, rather than the quest for transcendence through study of and submission to some external system of belief, is the most important for *Silence*. It involves two significant aspects. The first is an exploration of the nature of man's twofold consciousness, rational and nonrational, as in the poem "A Man Writes to a Part of Himself" and its companion poem "Depression." The second aspect of this theme of self-discovery involves Bly's exploration of the salutary correspondence between man and nature, as in the two poems "Poem in Three Parts" and "Hunting Pheasants in a Cornfield." Bly's psychospiritual, Jungian epic "Sleepers Joining Hands," published in 1973, is his most complete expression of this theme of the inward road.

The most prominent expression in *Silence* of the second theme, the ever-presence of the past in the present through the influence of the collective and personal unconscious on both the individual's and society's present behavior, occurs in the poem "Remembering in Oslo the Old Picture of the Magna Carta." The coordinates of conventional history, space and time, collapse in this poem's vision, for a "girl in a house dress" in modern Oslo "Is also the fat king" who signs the Magna Carta in the picture Bly remembers from his childhood. Similarly, Bly's own personal and ancestral past is ever-present and still influential in his psyche: "I too am still shocking grain, as I did as a boy, dog tired, / And my great-grandfather steps on his ship" (*Si*, 30) for his pioneer voyage to America. This theme becomes crucial to Bly's next book.

Bly's attraction to the detail of the ordinary things of this world is amply demonstrated throughout the book, especially in such poems as "Afternoon Sleep" and the often-anthologized short poems "Watering the Horse" and "In a Train." In the latter poem, four lines of haikulike enlightenment, the poet awakens on a train to the physical details of snow, darkness, and "the train window marked with soft dust." This scene, both in its detail and because of its associations through such by-now resonant *Silence* words as "snow," "darkness," and "dust," evokes from him unexpected depths of emotion, and he declares himself "utterly happy" (*Si*, 47). Throughout his career Bly has insisted on this strong physical basis for his imagery; his interfusion of the visible and invisible in the image creates the sense of powerful presence in his best poems. Bly elaborated on the theme of close observation of nature later in his career, especially in his prose poems and in his essays on the "thing" poems of Ponge and Rilke.

Bly's enduring theme, that of psychic exploration and self-discovery, manifests itself in two important aspects in *Silence*. The first depends on a definition of man as a creature possessing a twofold consciousness. Consciousness is awareness, and Bly believes that man possesses two sources of awareness: his rational, ego-consciousness (in Jung, unlike Freud, the ego is identical with all of consciousness), and his nonrational, personal, and collective unconscious. Man can and should, in fact must, recognize himself as a creature of twofold consciousness. He must listen to and learn from both sources of awareness, and he must bring them into creative alignment with each other. Many of the poems in *Silence* address this conception of human nature as consisting of twofold consciousness, though perhaps none so directly as the two companion poems "A Man Writes to a Part of Himself" and "Depression." The first, cited by one critic as "perhaps the most finely realized poem"[27] in the book, is one of a group of "marriage" poems in *Silence*. It is Bly's love letter to his anima, his soul, the unconscious counterpart to the masculine consciousness in his psyche, the balancing principle that the poet needs and longs for to make his personality whole. This poem expresses in an extended metaphor the effect of separating the masculine from the feminine, the conscious from the unconscious, in a person's psyche, whether man or woman. Bly personifies his anima as a wife who has been left uncared for and "starving" (*Si*, 36) in a cave; the ego, masculine in Bly's case because he is a man, may laugh in the daylight of conscious activity, but at night he is doomed to acknowledge his loneliness, a psychic loneliness, imaged as "a room of poverty / . . . a room with no heat." The poem's concluding questions are rhetorical, for obviously the separation hurts both sides, since they are inseparable—to repress or "hurt" one side of the psyche is to hurt one's self. An interesting aspect of this poem is its strong resemblance to a passage in Jung's *Memories, Dreams, Reflections*, where the psychologist talks of first discovering, then personifying, and even "writing letters to the anima,"[28] employing terms remarkably similar to Bly's in this poem.

Bly's companion poem to "A Man Writes to a Part of Himself" is titled "Depression." A less disguised psychological subject than the anima-as-wife, its three stanzas begin by describing the experience of panic, as in "my heart beats like an engine high in the air" (*Si*, 37), that may accompany depression. Then occurs the poet's dream of the nadir before an ascent to hope, signaled by the appearance of a mandala, an ancient and archetypal symbol of man's goal of psychospiritual wholeness mentioned often in Jung, "three work gloves, lying fingers to fingers, / In a circle, came towards me, and I awoke." Finally comes the effect of the experience and transformation, the poet's felt need to reestablish links with his unconscious, in "I want to go down and rest in the black silence of earth." This poem, like "A Man Writes to a Part of Himself," reveals Bly's Jungian inclinations. Both poems posit the existence of the conscious and unconscious parts of the psyche, and both poems declare that connecting with, reuniting, man's twofold consciousness is the road to health and wholeness. As Jung advocated, a person can be whole only through integration of both levels of consciousness, the light and the dark sides of the psyche.

A second major aspect of the theme of self-discovery in *Silence,* and in Bly's career, is the discovery of correspondence and mutual respect between man and nature. Bly's nature is not characterized as primarily noncity and noncivilized, as is customary in the pastoral tradition. Instead, Bly's nature symbolizes a part of mankind's evolutionary past, and therefore a part of his present psyche, which he needs to become conscious of in order to complete his own psychic development. Bly's nature provides a fundamental source of archetypal symbols to express the basic energies, the very processes, of man's own obscure, unconscious mind. In *Silence* the important aspect of this theme is the poet's discovering a relationship, a correspondence, between nature and human nature. "Poem in Three Parts" illustrates this process. With this poem Bly concludes the first section of his book, eleven "Poems of Solitude," and appropriately so. For this is a "call poem,"[29] which Bly defined as an appeal that nature sometimes makes to a person to "leave the house"[30] of ego-intellect, which all too often isolates man from nature and his own unconscious life. Bly's poet is called to seek out the ancient correspondences between himself and both the other creatures and the creative processes of Mother Nature.

Bly's "Poem in Three Parts" proceeds along this assumption of correspondence, beginning with the poet expressing his joy at waking up in the morning by celebrating his body, comparing himself-in-the-flesh to the "grass wrapped in its clouds of green" (*Si,* 21). In part 2 Bly again develops the man-nature correspondence by describing his nighttime journey of "long rides past castles and hot coals" as similar to the bath "in dark water" that the grass gets each night from the dew and the rain. Part 3 concludes the comparison, invoking nature's 'call" to the poet by the "plunging" leaves of the box-elder tree, a call to fuse with the natural cycle of life, death, and resurrection and "live forever, like the dust." The tone darkens as the poem develops, for the emotion of waking up and feeling like he could "live forever" gives way to the poet's final recognition that nature's forms are continually transforming themselves, and that if humans live forever it will be "like the dust," perhaps even as dust. Still, given Bly's belief in evolutionary psychology and the immortality of dreams and collective memory, living forever in a nonhuman form is a not unpleasant notion. The poem's conclusion is not meant as ironic, but profound: to be one with the dust is not to be less, but to be greater, than the ego/person traditionally conceived as apart from, and therefore supposedly superior to, nature.

A final poem from *Silence* expressing a similar concern for the correspondence between man and nature is "Hunting Pheasants in a Cornfield." Bly begins with a question, asking about his own attraction to a willow tree "alone in an open field" (*Si*, 14). Why is the poet's "body strangely torn, and cannot leave it," even when his rational mind dismisses the willow tree as a commonplace phenomenon? As the poem progresses, Bly's mind presents other reasons for not being interested in this tree, or in nature—the sun is cold and distant, the weeds died "long ago." But these images of alienation in space and time, like the subordination of the particular and physical by the rational intellect's preference for the general and abstract, are clearly specious, for the poet's "body," his nonrational, unconscious awareness, remains powerfully drawn to this willow.

The poet is "happy" lying under this willow tree, seeing it as a beacon, a guide for him "If I were a young animal ready to turn home at dusk." This final metaphor affirms subtly the real connection that exists between man and nature, man and the animals: Bly is a "young animal" himself, for he has followed a nonrational "body" attraction, a call, to this tree, to lie under it. Further, he has learned under the tree an ancient wisdom, the essential relationship of past and present through the influential presence of the collective unconscious, that record of the shared history of man and nature which each living person has possessed as humans evolved through the millenia. Both man and the tree participate in nature's processes, and Bly's discovery of this correspondence has taught him a truth about his own nature, his own soul.

The poet, in his late fifties, jailed after a political protest in Minnesota. Photograph courtesy of the Minneapolis Star and Tribune.

Chapter Three
The Challenge of Political Poetry: *The Light around the Body*

If *Silence in the Snowy Fields* belongs to the Minnesota-inwardness region in the geography of Robert Bly's imagination, then *The Light around the Body*[1] is best explained as poetry originating from a different region of the psyche, one shared with Bly the public persona—the editor/essayist of the *Fifties,* the publicly performing poet of the antiwar read-ins. Indeed, the very image of the psyche as a landscape whose landmarks have a shifting, rather than a fixed, relationship with each other, an image sanctioned by Bly's two mentors Jung and Neruda, is demonstrated by this book. As Jung declared, everyone has, in effect, several personalities within the psyche, since the individual's personality can best be described at any given stage of its individuation as the currently functioning relationship between such shifting elements of psyche as the ego, the shadow, and the persona. Bly uses a similar concept of personality in this book, even to employing the Jungian terms. Thus *Light* cannot be understood completely, either by itself or as part of the poet's literary career, without appreciating the poet's struggle in these poems to explore and chart a new region of his imagination's geography in response to the new challenge of the highly politicized times. There is significant evidence that Bly realized that an important subtext of the poetry in *Light* is the wrestling match between the poet's private, solitude-seeking face and its natural antagonist, the socially formed, public persona-mask. Thus *Light* is a record of Bly's artistic and personal struggle to achieve a new and functioning balance out of the opposition between the private, inward self of *Silence* and the public, outward self necessarily called forth to help him write and perform a public poetry on that most political of subjects, American society during the Vietnam War.

No matter how radical it may have seemed to the American academy's dominant tradition of the nonpolitical New Critics, Bly's was a centralist position when located within the entire spectrum[2] of possible relationships between art and politics in the Vietnam era. The antiwar movement was extremely broad-based, and writers, like other people, participated in it in a variety of ways, and from a variety of motives. Bly was more of an activist, less of a theoretician. His two antiwar anthologies, published by his own Sixties Press, display his catholic tastes in antiwar poetry; for Bly, political doctrine was less important than general moral outrage. In the movement, Bly's attitudes were similar to those of such traditional peace groups as the Quakers, the Unitarians (whose Beacon Press published both antiwar anthologies), and the antinuclear SANE. Bly's commitment to the inner world imbued him with an intense moral passion against the war, but he never espoused a particular political program for the outer world.

Of all the literature to come out of the Vietnam War, Bly's award-winning book of poetry stands as the best example of the dangers and possibilities inherent in the artist's attempt to create political art. For not only did Bly write a poetry that faced head on the thorniest issues surrounding the war, he did so with full consciousness of the very question of what it means to write political poetry. Not only in his writing for the *Sixties* during this period, but also in two major essays directly on the subject, "Leaping Up Into Political Poetry"[3] and "Giving to Johnson What is Johnson's,"[4] Bly provided arguments for the necessity of political poetry, as well as intelligent analyses of the dangers for both art and artist inherent in a situation where the artist is also a public partisan of the moral or political cause which his art addresses. Bly brought an honest, if impassioned, intelligence to bear on such New Criticism shibboleths as aesthetic distance, the intentional fallacy, and the universality of art. How emotionally detached must an artist be from his subject in order to present it in all its complexity? To what degree may he strive to persuade his audience before he imposes on their freedom of choice, before he stops creating art and starts making propaganda? What, finally, is the proper balance between the inward, psychological life and the external, political world? Bly's poetry and essays elucidate not only the essentially inward meaning of the poems in *Light,* but also these fundamental questions facing any poet who accepts the challenge to write about his life in the broadest meaning of that word.

"Leaping Up into Political Poetry," which introduced the antiwar anthology *Forty Poems Touching on Recent American History,* addresses several major aspects of political poetry by explaining its relationship to Bly's enduring theme of inwardness. Bly begins his important essay by bemoaning the fact that in America, unlike Europe and South America, "most educated people advise that poetry on political subjects should not be attempted" (*F*, 7), that neither man's "finest awareness" nor "human sensitivity" are capable of understanding politics. Bly sees in this attitude evidence that society and its institutions, such as high school, churches, television, and advertising, may be engaged in a "calculated effort . . . to kill awareness" (*F*, 9), to smother Americans' sense of the essential inwardness of their lives. Bly takes as axiomatic the starting point of his argument justifying outward, political poetry as a function of the inward, individual life: "It's clear that many of the events that create our foreign relations and our domestic relations come from more or less hidden impulses in the American psyche" (*F*, 10). Indeed, this statement provides the underlying thesis for all the poetry in *Light*.

Bly's essay declares that "the poet's main job" is to break through the outward husk in which American society has encased the psyche of both poet and nonpoet. Therefore, the writing of political poetry must be just "like the writing of personal poetry, a sudden drive by the poet inward" (*F*, 10), so that the poet "can speak of inward and political things with the same assurance" (*F*, 10). Bly attacks the "political activists in the literary world" (*F*, 10) who try to produce political poetry by pushing poets into political events, making them "abandon privacy." For Bly, "the truth is that the political poem comes out of the deepest privacy" (*F*, 11), not out of subordination of the inward, individual life to external political events. Both types of poetry have similar goals, for the "true political poem does not order us either to take specific acts: like the personal poem, it moves to deepen awareness" (*F*, 13).

The way for the poet to create such political poetry is to write in a language that entangles some of the national psyche in his personal poem, and thus to make his readers newly aware of the national, hence political psyche. Bly invokes Yeats's word "entangles" (*F*, 11) to speak of the poet's language capturing indirectly some of the substance of his political life in his personal poems. Bly insists that poets who claim to be "not political," especially when they live in a time such as the sixties, when politics so infused all aspects of life, are indulging in "a fiction" (*F*, 12). Bly asks the reader to imagine the "life of the nation" (*F*, 12) as a sphere floating above everyone, as well as something deep within each individual. To leap up into this sphere of the nation's life, into political poetry, the poet has to be confident enough on the inward level that he can abandon his own ego-concerns and enter another, larger psyche. Thus both a drive inward, in order to awaken confidence in his inner self, and a leap upward, in order to engage in, to explore, and to entangle the larger, political life of his nation in his own consciousness, are necessary for the poet to write successful political poetry.

Bly specifically counsels against several kinds of threats posed by political subjects to the artist and the success of his art. The first threat Bly warns against is writing out of overwhelming emotions such as "hatred, or fear" (F, 13). Because he believes in a close relationship between the poem and the poet's psyche, he also believes that poetry written out of such emotions has the same disastrous effect on the poet as it does on the poem, just as an act of aggression hurts not only the victim but also the aggressor. Bly makes this point throughout *Light,* as well as in his essay "Giving to Johnson What Is Johnson's," the preface to a second anthology, *A Poetry Reading against the Vietnam War,* where he notes that a "really serious evil of the war, rarely discussed, is the harm it will do the Americans inwardly" (P, 7). This becomes the major theme of Bly's longest Vietnam poem, "The Teeth Mother Naked at Last."

Two other common forms of falsely political poetry are the personal poem masquerading as political because it records a poet's private opinion about a political subject, and the impersonal catalogue of political assertions, typical of propaganda and much of the European anti-American sloganeering of the Vietnam period. The first, prevalent in the American thirties, invariably fails to entangle the two worlds, and thus fails to engage the political issue as anything greater than a matter of individual opinion. The second is certainly political but fails the test as poetry because the poet's own psyche is too distanced from it. That is, it is not personal enough, not truly inward, and thus unconvincing cant, mere "rhetoric" (F, 13). Bly concludes his analysis of flawed political poetry with a lengthy discussion of several examples of successful political poetry. The most important is a poem by Pablo Neruda, "The Dictators." American examplars include William Vaughn Moody, Thomas McGrath, Kenneth Rexroth, and Robert Duncan.

There are other important issues regarding the relationship of the artist to the art of political poetry. In Bly's case, a relevant question is what effect his intense, public career as a critic, not only of politics but also of other poets, had on his judgment as a poet. Bly's political poetry began before the Vietnam War period, and included a collection titled *For the Ascension of J. P. Morgan* which no one would publish because it was too political for the Eisenhower fifties (*T*, 10–11). Further, by the time *Light* appeared Bly had not only translated the work and analyzed the experience of a master of political poetry, the Chilean Pablo Neruda,[5] but had also served as the very busy and highly visible co-founder of American Writers Against the Vietnam War. His extensive experience with politics and poetry had prepared Bly uniquely to write the best poetry of the Vietnam period; but it had also encouraged the overdevelopment of a public persona in an individual who had been devoted to solitude and inwardness all his life. If Vietnam had never happened, Bly would have found another form of expression for his developing persona. But perhaps Bly's intense preoccupation with criticism during this period had a deleterious effect on his poetry by strengthening excessively his public persona.[6] Bly himself described such a threat of the overdeveloped persona dominating the inward self by quoting Jung's reference to "spiritual inflation" (*T*, 125–26), both an expansion and a cheapening of the psychic life. Bly many times swore that all he wanted from his political poetry was to increase awareness in the audience, not to make them agree with him or move them to action. But when his political poems overreach (and his quasi-political criticism too, as in the case of his attack on James Dickey),[7] it is because he demands too much—he wants agreement, allegiance, and even specific actions against the enemies of his position. Perhaps Bly's personal lesson from the antiwar movement was learning to integrate and thereby moderate the role of his persona in his psyche.

Bly's extensive analyses of the dangers of political poetry should not overshadow the tremendous allure its possibilities held for him and for the majority of his sixties contemporaries. The two main attractions were the chance to make poetry relevant again and the artists' desire to share in and capture the major energies of their time, which in the sixties were the sociopolitical energies. Very few, if any, works of art better capture the spirit of the Vietnam War period than Robert Bly's poetry in *Light*. Surely, Bly's book has many claims on the success accorded it by the judges of the 1968 National Book Award: "If we poets had to chose something that would be for us our Address on the State of the Nation, it would be this book."[8] Bly deserves

credit for the best poetry dealing directly with the complex sociopolitical themes of the Vietnam period. It is a curious fact that many
people today have either forgotten or never knew (many had not even
been born) that the sixties was given its particular shape precisely because it was played out against the backdrop of the Vietnam War.
All the exotica of acid, acid rock, communes, hippies, etc., would
not have loomed so large and garish without the magnifying back-
lighting of wartime to push their forms toward the grotesque. The
Vietnam War was not a function of the sixties' sociopolitical attitudes, but the other way around. The pervasive mood of psychic dislocation caused by the war's disruption of everyone's lives, from the
Selective Service draft all the way to the extremes of death in a rice
paddy or on a college lawn at Kent State, unsettled a Baby Boom
generation just coming to maturity in 1964, only twenty years after
their own fathers had fought and perhaps even died proudly in World
War II. Further, the profound moral uncertainty about the rightness
of the war created a climate in which philosophies such as "tune in,
turn on, drop out" (Timothy Leary's oft-quoted dictum) seemed for a
time to be both viable and even honorable. Ambivalence about the
war permeated American society, even to the highest levels of government. A top-secret memo from Secretary of Defense Robert MacNa-
mara to President Lyndon Johnson, written in 1967 but only made
public in 1984, speaks of "a costly distortion in the American national consciousness" created by the "picture of the world's greatest
superpower killing or seriously injuring 1,000 noncombatants a
week, while trying to pound a tiny backward nation into submission
on an issue whose merits are hotly disputed."[9] When the institutions
failed, the country looked elsewhere for answers. If a poet's relevance
should be measured in terms of "how thoroughly or how completely
he or she negotiates what all must face,"[10] then Bly's facing up to
the Vietnam War period in *Light* is an important testament to his
achievement of redefining the role of the American poet for his time.

Speaking in Two Languages: Poetic Strategies in *Light*

In *Light* Bly attempts to "speak in two languages," to the issues of
both the "outward man" and the "inward man," as he declares in his
epigraph to the book's first section. Bly addresses such major "outward," sociopolitical themes of the period as the pernicious effects on

American society of the lust for money and power, the general social malaise fostered by the unresponsiveness of government to the citizens, and the racism endemic in American society from the country's founding to the present, especially as it reveals itself in the subconscious motives for the Vietnam War. But Bly's poetry, as always, looked deeper than the sociopolitical level, and sought to establish a basis for universality in its analysis of social problems as emanating from "inward," psychic, problems whose only cure could be increased awareness and what Bly called "the slow struggle to improve character."[11] In *Light* Bly consistently bases the historical/political dimension of human action upon the ontological/psychological dimension, even in poems which at first reading seem to be only about sociopolitical problems. Thus the poetry of *Light* finally posits the perfection of the outer world upon the improvement of the inner world, the soul of the individual. This overarching theme of *Light* is reinforced by Bly's rearrangement of poems for the British edition, which toned down the sociopolitical thrust of the American edition and emphasized the theme of the psychological development of consciousness and character as the fundamental key to social progress.

Bly altered other elements of his poetics to achieve the radical change in his voice necessary for the public poems of *Light*. The change most immediately obvious to the reader familiar with *Silence* is the mordant note of Juvenalian satire with which Bly barely contains the bitter hostility of his voice in many of the poems. Although no more than half the poems of *Light* mention Vietnam, the others seem inevitably colored by the pervasive psychic background of wartime. Perhaps the most famous example of Bly's deeply satirical tone is "Counting Small-Boned Bodies," whose ironic opening line of "Let's count the bodies over again" develops intensity as the poem builds toward Bly's final, fascistic image of a corpse so small it could fit "into a finger-ring, for a keepsake forever."

Bly embellishes and enlarges his satiric, public voice in *Light* by imaginatively invoking elements used in their public performance—whether poetry readings or antiwar read-ins. Bly became famous for his incorporation of music, dance, and masks into his performance of his poems from memory for many audiences.[12] The poetry written on the page seems influenced by the knowledge that it would be performed. For instance, not only the public tone but also poetic lines which sometimes seem, when eye-read, flaccid, prosaic, or unpunctuated, sound fine when presented accompanied by the intonations, pauses, gestures, and even music a speaking, performing poet has at his command. This is especially true of poems which are in-character (and caricature) performance pieces, such as "The Busy Man Speaks," "Three Presidents," and "Andrew Jackson's Speech."

A third poetic strategy used effectively by Bly in both *Light* and other books is to make a statement through the arrangement of his poems. He had done this earlier in *Silence*. Both American and British editions of *Light* contain the same poems, unchanged, yet the different arrangement in the two editions makes one significantly different from the other. Bly has stated, in correspondence with the author, that he made the changes "just because I had a *chance* to: the American ed. is a political book, emphasizing events in the *outer* world, so to speak."[13] The changes recast the goal of the journey/struggle of the book as not simply the perfecting of society but also, even primarily, the perfecting of the individual psyche. Unlike the earlier American edition, in the British edition there is no mention of Vietnam after the first section (which is exactly the first half of the book). Moving all the Vietnam poems to the first half of the book allows Bly to concentrate the social and political protest poetry in one part, then gradually modulate his anger, and the book's momentum, toward a qualified hopefulness based on his recognition of the ultimate primacy of the inward life. The poems of sections 2 and 3 are spoken by one who has been profoundly affected, but not overwhelmed, by the Vietnam experience. Thus Bly has chosen to create a more balanced book by rearranging the poems for the British edition.

But Bly's most important strategy in *Light* involves the use of the historical/psychological image. This is a continuation and extension of the deep image that played so central a role in the poems of *Silence*. Just as the deep image was intended to allow the poet's unconscious to speak to the reader's unconscious, so the historical/psychological image in *Light* is intended to allow the present to speak to the past, and vice versa. Its validity derives from Jung's notion that each person contains in his psyche a memory of mankind's experiences, so that "the form of the world into which he is born is already inborn in him as a virtual image,"[14] making him in a sense familiar with what he sees for the first time. Bly's image in *Light* is often a variety of historical allusion, a direct invocation of some past event to comment on the present, as in "Hearing Men Shout at Night on Mac-Dougal Street": "The street is a sea, and mud boils up / When the anchor is lifted, for now at midnight there is about to sail / The first New England slave-ship with the Negroes in the hold." But rather than an Eliotic, ironic contrast between glorious past and decadent present, Bly intends the reader to see here in the final lines a causal, psychic connection between past and present, here between contemporary street violence (perhaps even riots) and the slave trade to which the self-righteous yet middle-class, materialistic Puritan conscience accommodated itself.

A second important referent for Bly's historical/psychological imagery, not so obvious as the previous one, is well illustrated in "Suddenly Turning Away." In this poem Bly images contemporary human values by alluding to theories of their origin in the major stages of human and even prehuman evolution, stages believed to be physically encoded, and thus still operative, in three layers of the human brain,[15] namely, the reptile brain, the mammal brain, and the neocortex or what Bly called the "new" brain. Whatever the scientific merits of such theories, they provide useful metaphors for the poet. Such a brain structure would seem to support Jung's concept of a collective unconscious, the inherited "wisdom and experience of uncounted centuries, which are laid down in its [the psyche's] archetypal organs."[16] In Bly's poem, the reptile brain, with its instinctual control of primitive emotions such as hatred and self-preservation, seizes control over the mammal brain and its associated values of affection and friendship, in these lines: "Someone comes near, the jaw / Tightens, bullheads bite / The snow, moments of intimacy waved away." The bullhead is a catfish, a creature associated with the transition from sea to land in human evolutionary development. Bly images the betrayal of our human potential that occurs when these "shadows / Of not-love come" and the reptile brain, with its emotions of fear and hatred, takes over; he uses an historical/psychological image of the new brain, with its radiant energy, coupled with an image of the human unconscious to represent what happens: "The gold discs / Fall from our ears. / The sea grows cloudy." The "gold discs" are perhaps the golden circles painted on the Buddha to show where enlightenment can enter the soul; the cloudy sea images the relationship between consciousness and unconscious when one is under the sway of this lower, reptilian emotion—murky and confused, not clear, not harmonized, less than fully human. Images such as "bullheads" and "gold discs" are scarcely allusions, since they are so obscure; yet as descriptive, connotative images within the context of the poem, they speak to the reader.

The image of "bullheads bite / the snow" is one of many animal images that Bly uses to weave a totemic tapestry. Bly had admired similar uses of animal imagery in other poets, especially Lorca (*T*, 4–7). In this book of ostensibly political poetry Bly manages to include images of ants, moles, horses, dogs, toads, turkeys, snails, bulls, bullheads, and turtles—and all of these creatures have associations with man's evolutionary past and therefore his personality and politics in the present. Perhaps a Jungian might have predicted that a poet so given over to the concerns of society and the persona would necessarily generate such a balancing, compensatory movement toward the shadow side of the psyche.[17] In *Light* both the animal imagery and the historical imagery provide contexts Bly draws upon to give depth and psychic inwardness to poems whose ostensible themes are those of the outward, sociopolitical man.

Three Poetic Voices in *Light*

There are three broad types of political poem to be found in *Light*, illustrating three very different approaches to a major problem of political poetry: how to establish an artistically successful relationship between the poet's political theme and intent and his persona, whether the voice/person he is or consciously creates to speak a particular poem. In the first type, the poet builds his political theme upon personal experience or reflection. In the second type the poet assumes the persona of a satiric visionary who comments on publicly known problems and situations. In the third, and least successful, type the poet neither builds nor keeps within a satiric persona, but instead speaks out as an overwrought partisan whose words draw more attention to the speaker than to his poem. The problem these types address is central not only to all political poetry, especially Bly's, but also to the whole region of Bly's imagination responsible for the *Fifties* as well as *Light*. Indeed, one might locate it at the core of the complex in Bly's psyche that dominates his literary personality from 1966–1972, from his early Vietnam poetry and his work as co-founder of American Writers Against the Vietnam War, to the publication of "Sleepers Joining Hands," the long meditative poem that signals his farewell to political poetry. A comparison of the relative success Bly has in each of these three types of relationship between the artist and the political poem will help explain the good and the bad poetry in *Light,* illuminating some of the reasons why one poem works and another doesn't.

The best political poems in *Light,* at least for eye-reading from a book rather than hearing at one of Bly's celebrated performance-readings, are of the type illustrated by "Sleet Storm on the Merritt Parkway" and the ironically understated "Counting Small-Boned Bodies." In "Sleet Storm" Bly succeeds in three important areas. First, his voice develops a convincing authority within the poem by building from within, rather than arguing from some external moral authority. Second, the images interrelate and grow within the poetic context, rather than existing separately in an asserted, undeveloped list. Finally, because of Bly's skill in handling the first two problems, the political theme emerges as integral with the personal life of the poem and poet, and so is more convincing to the reader. A closer look will illustrate Bly's craft in these three aspects of his poetics:

> I look out at the white sleet covering the still streets
> As we drive through Scarsdale—
> The sleet began falling as we left Connecticut,
> And the winter leaves swirled in the wet air after cars
> Like hands suddenly turned over in a conversation.
> Now the frost has nearly buried the short grass of March.
> Seeing the sheets of sleet untouched on the wide streets,
> I think of the many comfortable homes stretching for miles,
> Two and three stories, solid, with polished floors,
> With white curtains in the upstairs bedrooms,
> And small perfume flagons of black glass on the window sills,
> And warm bathrooms with guest towels, and electric lights—
> What a magnificent place for a child to grow up!
> And yet the children end in the river of price-fixing,
> Or in the snowy field of the insane asylum.
> The sleet falls—so many cars moving toward New York—
> Last night we argued about the Marines invading Guatemala
>   in 1947,
> The United Fruit Company had one water spigot for 200
>   families,
> And the ideals of America, our freedom to criticize,
> The slave systems of Rome and Greece, and no one agreed.

Bly begins "Sleet Storm" by asserting his identity as the voice of the poem; yet by the conclusion the individual "I" has skillfully merged itself into the collective "we," enlarging the poem's political significance as well as its poetic resonance. The poet's "I" has grown to speak convincingly as the voice of everyman—the poet, his friends, and the reader too.

Similarly, "Sleet Storm" succeeds, where other poems fail, in establishing its emergent form; it builds the poem's key image of the "sleet storm" out of its own poetic context, without depending so crucially upon allusion to other, less accessible contexts such as cross-cultural mother symbols or the three-brain theory. The "sleet" of the poem's title begins as a fact in a realistic scene, but then builds through repetition and association. The "sheets of sleet" covering the "Merritt" road remind the poet of the materialistic, surface comfort of the middle-class life-style, whose seeming perfection so often covers a spiritual neglect which, as in the psychodynamic of the inevitable return of the repressed, has the power to erupt and profoundly transform the individual's psyche. Bly expresses this shocking transformation by metamorphosing the sleet storm into a striking image of the twisted inward life, into "the snowy field of the insane asylum." All the resonances from this major symbol of Bly's first book, where snow was identified with the silent but powerfully benevolent presence of the inward life, are reversed here to make a very strong statement. How is it, the poet asks, that children raised in such a comfortable environment can "end up in the river of price-fixing," committing spiritual suicide for money? This phenomenon echoes the epigraph from Freud to this section of *Light:* "What a distressing contrast there is between the radiant intelligence of the child, and the feeble mentality of the average adult."

Because this successful poem allows both the voice and the imagery to develop within its own context, the thematic balance between the personal world and the political world is convincingly drawn. Unlike many of the more overtly political poems in *Light,* "Sleet Storm on the Merritt Parkway" establishes a fundamental basis for the reader's being interested in politics: his own self-interest, his own life. The theme of this poem is twofold. Most immediately, the poem speaks of the failure that can befall both the individual and the nation when they refuse to acknowledge the complexity of human personality, especially its basis in the personal and collective unconscious life, and

instead adopt a materialistic, pragmatic philosophy, especially its often tragic corollary that Scarsdale is heaven and money is merit. But
the second aspect of the poem's theme is that individual behavior in
the personal sphere corresponds to, reflects, and illuminates the individual's political behavior, whether through his active participation or
passive acceptance of the behavior of the various political entities of
which he is perforce a member. This is the meaning of the last four
lines of the poem, in which Bly links the ethical confusion of personal
values, where middle-class children "end in the river of price-fixing,"
with a corresponding ethical confusion over political values. The earlier image of "hands suddenly turned over in conversation" had associated the sleet storm with the poet's anger and exasperation at the
inability, or refusal, of a group of people successful enough in America's meritocracy to live in Connecticut's "comfortable homes" to
agree about such seemingly straightforward issues as the conflict between "the ideals of America" and the "slave systems of Rome and
Greece." For Bly, the personal is not so easily separated from the political as his middle-class friends claim; though in this poem, unlike
later ones, he is careful not to insist on an easily understood, simplistic cause-and-effect relationship between the two.

A second type of political poem found in *Light,* one different in
voice and image from "Sleet Storm," is seen in "After the Industrial
Revolution, All Things Happen at Once." In this poem Bly's artistic
persona adopts the dispassionate tone of a satirical visionary, speaking
from the beginning as both "we" and "I," inviting the reader to "enter a strange world" where the past is still present and the American
Revolution has not been won. Here Bly's artistic persona is not so
much building an emotionally convincing argument as embellishing
on an accepted fact, the unceasing struggle between the individual
and big business/big government, from the American Revolution to
the present. The poet uses historical allusions to demonstrate his
Hegelian theme of progress through dialectical opposition: the American spirit of revolution will live just as long as its dialectical opposite, the spirit of pragmatic materialism, is a threat to individual
values. Bly's historical images of revolution include Washington, the
Whiskey Rebellion, the miners of Cripple Creek, and Coxey's army.
Historical images of materialism begin with the mercenary Hessian
army which Washington defeated by marching on Christmas day.
Others include the two Henry Cabot Lodges, both associated with

commercially motivated American attacks on Cuba (who says history doesn't repeat itself?); Henry Ford, inventor of the assembly line as well as the "history is bunk" line; and Charlie Wilson, Eisenhower's secretary of defense and former chairman of General Motors, well-known in his day for using government to further the interests of big business, on his oft-satirized belief that "What's good for General Motors is good for America."

The force of the poem's prophetic persona, not a patterned, incremental poetic context, holds these allusions together. However, the allusions themselves are not impossibly obscure, nor is the reader forced to make any greater emotional commitment to them than it takes to appreciate their role as part of someone else's satire. Thus Bly's use of an impersonal, prophetic persona here actually defuses the partisan emotionalism that undercuts some of his other political poems, such as "Turning Away from Lies." The reader feels the visionary persona is appropriate for the political subject, much as the dream vision is right for that labor movement song "Joe Hill," popular in the sixties. The poem's return to the "Whiskey Boys" of stanza one in its conclusion rounds off the poetic structure. The last stanza's image of "singing" is meant to demonstrate the power of the past speaking through the visionary speaker to the present, singing in unison with it, supporting the spirit of the many protest marches and protest songs of the sixties. Both vision and song are here ways of mediating the intensity of the persona's emotion.

The third and least convincing type of political poetry in *Light* fails because it leans too heavily upon the self-assertive emotion and authority of the poet as partisan. "Turning Away From Lies," mawkish and prosaic at times, comes perilously close to parodying the confessional poetry that Bly consistently criticized as too ego-oriented. The voice speaking lines such as "When shall I have peace? Peace this way and peace that way?" (perhaps inspired by the equally maudlin song "Give Peace a Chance") is certainly not the transparent "I" of the best poems of *Silence,* nor the controlled public voice of the best political poems of *Light.* Seldom does Bly get less poetic or more preachy (the entire second stanza is a catalog of prosaic subject-verb statements virtually devoid of poetry) than in the penultimate line of stanza 2: "No one in business can be a Christian." Bly's earlier criticism of catalogs of opinion that fail as political poetry because "the poem is not inside the poet's own life (*F*, 12) might be fairly applied here. The poem's flaws can be traced back to a common cause, the excessive emotional assertiveness of the poet's voice, and the concomitant desertion of his inward life.

Balancing the Two Worlds:
A Reading of *The Light around the Body*

While the political poetry is the new element in Bly's repertoire showcased in *Light,* there are good reasons to believe that it was never meant to dominate the poetry of inwardness that makes up a large part of the book. The title should be considered the book's most important directive. It firmly turns the reader's attention to Bly's enduring theme of man's twofold consciousness, here imaged as the body and the "light around the body." This trope, obviously, is neither sociological nor political, but psychological. That Bly chose it for the book's title underscores his commitment to the pursuit of the inward road, even during this period of his most intense public, political activity, both as poet and man. Taken from the poem "Looking Into a Face," this title image refers to a new state of consciousness achieved by the poet through "conversation" with another person, through wandering "in a face," not through overt social or political action. Further, Bly's psychoreligious imagery associates this new state of consciousness with a spiritual resurrection; as Bly declares, "I have risen to a body / Not yet born." Throughout his career Bly uses traditional religious language and imagery to describe a state of being that is essentially inward and psychological, not political. Finally, Bly's emphasis on the inward is clear from his strategy in the British edition to rearrange the poems to integrate the sociopolitical with the psychological in a balance that represents his own sense of their appropriate relationship.

However, in 1967 the political poetry of the American edition's first three sections was a new kind of work, both for Bly and for America, and no one who read the book when it first appeared doubted that politics, especially anti-Vietnam politics, was primary in the poet's imagination. Now, removed by time from the passion of the Vietnam period, the reader of *Light* can better understand just how pervasively Bly related his many sociopolitical themes to the pursuit of the inward road of self-development, which he had introduced as the major theme of his life's work in *Silence.* A close reading of the poems of the American *Light's* five sections will demonstrate that the intent of the book was from the beginning not only to acknowledge the two worlds, the personal and the political, but also to explore and affirm the intergral relationship between them.

"The Two Worlds"

The theme of section 1, "The Two Worlds," is the threat to the inward, spiritual world posed by various aspects of the outward, materialistic world. The presence of the inward world is easily recognized in the poems of this section, perhaps because the most overpowering aspect of Bly's outer world, the Vietnam War, appears in only one of the poems. The first poem, "The Executive's Death," announces this theme in its opening line: "Merchants have multiplied more than the stars of heaven," while "half the population" slumber inwardly, in a kind of death of the soul. The executive, ruler of this society, is also dying, and his dream of his own death symbolizes its cause: "cut off and dying, / A pine stump talks to him of Goethe and Jesus." The poem's final turn links the commuter society with the executive's death, using images of blindness ("like moles") and fear ("hares flying") to suggest their inward state. Bly builds on his earlier image of the population sleeping like grasshoppers by concluding the poem with the appropriate musical accompaniment for such a non-leaping, uninspired spiritual state, the dull commuter train "sound of thousands of small wings."

The threat posed by business to the inward spirit of the business man, as well as to whomever else his actions affect, is the theme of Bly's Menippean satire of a social stereotype in "The Busy Man Speaks." Using a dramatic monologue, sometimes wearing a scary Halloween mask when performing the poem, Bly has a stereotypical businessman reveal himself as an enemy of "mother" consciousness, Jung's anima, and as a fanatic for the values of patriarchal consciousness. The businessman has been confirmed by "an arm of flame" from "the Chase National Bank" in a religion dedicated to "money," to the "perfect gestures" and unceasing "cheerfulness" of total self-repression, and to dominance of nature by numbers, imaged as "the landscape of zeros." These values and images associated with mother and father consciousness are developed more fully as aspects of the inward life in Bly's next book, *Sleepers*. Here they refer equally to the inward and outward worlds.

"Johnson's Cabinet Watched by Ants" adds new elements to the conflict between inward and outward worlds. In this poem Bly links the government with the business community and establishment religion, and he introduces images that entangle the Vietnam War for the first time in the book in the struggle between the two worlds. By day the president, his ministers, his generals, and businessmen talk of principles; by night they revel in betraying them. The excitement of their betrayal is an important motif for Bly's work; the inward and outward worlds are inextricably linked, so that when one betrays the other, there is both a cause and an effect in each world. In stanza 3 this display of revelry in hypocrisy is watched by ants and toads, emblems of an older stage of evolution, but one that seems to be manifesting itself in Johnson and his minions. The ants sing songs about a psychodynamic that led to tyranny long before America and Johnson, and the toads respond out of a primitive, instinctual love for the excitement of dominance. For Bly these emotions of power-lust and betrayal are legacies from the most primitive stages of human evolution.

The final poem of this section reaffirms the primacy of the inward life, even as it recapitulates in significant ways the conflicts between outer and inner worlds presented in the previous poems of the section. "Romans Angry about the Inner World" links the ancient antagonists of Jesus, the Christians, and "our mother / In the other world" with the modern "executives" of both business and government who were the chief antagonists of the inner world in earlier poems. In Bly's poetry and prose, imperial Rome symbolizes a society in which the state is the enemy of art, of the individual, and especially of the anima and its associated mother consciousness values.[18] Bly's Rome is an image of what America could become if it continues on the imperial road it has taken in Vietnam. The poem's first line is affirmative of the enduring power of the inner world against the outer. Since every child is born with a knowledge of the joy of the inner world, how can the social forces of the outer world ever obliterate the inner world without obliterating themselves? Bly himself is angry as he describes the Romans torturing a woman out of hatred and fear of their own inner, mother spirit. They are "astonished" when nature shows sympathy for the woman by covering her mangled body with "A light snow." Bly's anger, expressed through two exclamations in the poem's final lines, gives way to an ominous prophetic curse that is fulfilled elsewhere in Bly's poetry, in "The Teeth Mother Naked at Last." Here the inner world is imaged as a vengeful fury, returning to destroy and thereby triumph over those Romans/

executives who had repressed her: "It is like a jagged stone / Flying toward them out of the darkness." Again, the sociopolitical problems of the outer world find their solution in an act of the inner world. Thus the book's first section, "The Two Worlds," concludes with a sense of the primacy of the inner world over the outer.

"The Various Arts of Poverty and Cruelty"

Section 2 in the American edition of *Light* presents a deepening and intensification of the poet's dejection at the sociopolitical problems of his time. Unlike section 1, section 2 does not hint at any possibility of redemption, either for society or for the poet who lives in that society. Bly's vision sees only a twisted and disturbed inward life. It is as if the more important of man's two worlds has been irrevocably lost. The section begins with "Come with Me," a poem of ironic invitation to enter "into those things that have felt this despair for so long." Section 2, titled "The Various Arts of Poverty and Cruelty," then proceeds through a virtual catalog of sociopolitical problems (with the notable exception of the major problem, the Vietnam War, which is saved for section 3) and their concomitant relationship to the inward life. Section 2 concludes with an image of final despair in "Sleet Storm on the Merritt Parkway," the failure of the poet's own circle of friends to reach agreement even on society's problems, let alone the solutions.

The most important theme that holds together the poems of section 2 is the relationship between government and the people. Bly is interested in the ways in which the government is a creature of the people's inward life. Even when government takes actions found repulsive to many, such as lying to the people, does it not somehow find sanction for these in socioeconomic cultural patterns, the unspoken attitudes and values of many of the governed, the group Nixon called "the silent majority"? If all of life is a piece, a seamless garment, then the government's action in some way reflects the will of many of the governed—not necessarily the conscious political will, but the unconscious, psychological will of the collective American soul. This is the implicit theme of many of these poems, and it is based on the assumption of an integral though often obscure relationship between the inward and outward worlds.

"Come with Me" begins this theme by imaging the despair of the citizens as the debris of the American highway: "removed Chevrolet wheels," "shredded inner tubes," and "curly steel shavings . . . on garage benches" are like men "Who have given up, and blame everything on the government." Bly presents the common citizen's attitude of seeing the government not only as unresponsive to but also separate from, even a scapegoat for, human failure as itself a form of failure. Throughout the poem the images of the material world are linked to corresponding images of the inner world through personification. The last line underscores this linkage by expressing the inner-outer despair with a variation on Bly's favorite symbol of the inward life, the road. He invites the reader to "come with me" not only into the wreckage of cars that have tried the road and failed, but into the despair of the very road itself. The road's failure symbolizes modern man's psychic failure to have a destination, or even to connect one thing to another, like "those roads in South Dakota that feel around in the darkness. . . ."

"The Great Society" takes its title from President Lyndon Johnson's name for his vision of America under his administration. The poem presents the sadness of history endlessly repeating itself, rather than progressing. Bly sees history as depending, finally, as much on the ever-present unconscious dynamics of the collective human psyche as it does on the shifting alignment of forces in the conscious, sociopolitical sphere. The ironies of evolutionary history include the fact that its product, man, denies it: "Hands developed with terrible labor by apes / Hang from the sleeves of evangelists" who preach creationism. People forget, or become separated from their collective past: modern suburban man waters his lawn "even in the rain," and the crown-shaped marquees of movie theaters pay unconscious tribute to the "murdered kings" whose death freed the symbol of monarchy for popular, democratic co-opting. Johnson's program for "the great society" is belied by such betrayals of past achievments, just as it was by his own "dreams of invading Cuba," proof that he has learned nothing from a mistake made twice before by American presidents. The theme of the poem is the betrayal of political progress by inward, psychological failure, as imaged in the final line, where "the mayor sits with his head in his hands."

Psychologizing the Presidency

If the government is "of the people" in a psychological sense, then the most obvious symbol of this relationship for Bly is the president himself, elected not only for a political platform but also as an image of personality that finds a resonance in the national psyche. Further, the president's personality often has more to do with his policies than does his platform; and both personal and political dimensions of the presidency combine in an amalgam that itself becomes added to the collective character of the national psyche. By envisioning the president as a creation of the people who elect him, Bly thus bypasses "the left wing orthodoxy which sees the war as simply a ruling-class plot, as if the ruling class did not have the support of a large portion of the population."[19] Bly treats this theme directly in several poems in this section, including "Three Presidents," "Andrew Jackson's Speech," and "Listening to President Kennedy Lie about the Cuban Invasion," as well as indirectly in "The Great Society" and "The Current Administration." Bly presents the presidency as a microcosm of the complex relationship between the external political world and the individual psychic life in America, as well as between history and the present in the collective American psyche. In "Three Presidents" Bly uses three imagined monologues by Jackson, Teddy Roosevelt, and John Kennedy to suggest the symbolism of their presidencies in psychological, rather than political, terms.

Bly's Jackson is the American romantic who imagines himself as "a white horse," the classic symbol of righteousness from that quintessentially American romantic genre, the Western movie. In his acceptance speech for the National Book Award for *Light,* Bly explained the symbolism of Andrew Jackson, calling him "the General Westmoreland of 1830," involved in a war against the Indians, and "recommending murder of a race as a prudent policy" (*T,* 106). Jackson also brought to the presidency a willingness to use the force of government to quell protests against it. As he says in "Andrew Jackson's Speech," the "Republic lies in the blossoms of Washington," not in the souls of the American people. For Bly, Jackson's flaw is the romantic's failing of identifying too closely with his beloved, admitting no criticism of her, and thereby shutting off any possibility of reform and improvement. In "Andrew Jackson's Speech" Bly links Jackson with Aeneas, who preferred Rome to Dido, as two men who looked at an all-consuming passion and misunderstood its nature. Jackson's speech advocating shooting people to save the government is one side, in the sixties the wrong side, of the argument about who is the government, about who are referred to in the Founding Fathers' phrase "of the people": the bureaucrats in Washington or the citizens of the land. The sixties' ongoing national debate about civil disobedience is the thread that links the civil rights movement to the antiwar demonstrations, the two most important sociopolitical movements of that decade. As Bly declared in his 1968 acceptance of the National Book Award, an occasion on which he himself defied the law, including J. Edgar Hoover's FBI agents in the audience, by turning over his $1000 prize to a draft resister, "no one needs to be ashamed of the acts of civil disobedience committed in the tradition of Thoreau" (*T*, 107). Both the Vietnam War and the sixties' inner city riots in Detroit, Washington, D.C., and the Watts section of Los Angeles have proved simplistic Jackson's, Hoover's, and Westmoreland's romantic response of law and order at all costs.

The second president invoked in Bly's poem about the presidency is Theodore Roosevelt, portrayed as full of bluff and bluster ("I crushed snails with my bare teeth"), eager to be perceived as the epitome of both political and personal power. Roosevelt is an enemy of nature, willing to rearrange it to suit man's needs. In his personal life Roosevelt is also an enemy of the values Bly associates with the mothers in the earlier poem "The Busy Man Speaks." Roosevelt's psychological state is revealed through his desire to "be a stone" with no cracks in it, to be a stone that holds the conscious life aloof from the unconscious, like "a stone that holds up the edge of the lake house." But Bly shows the fallacy of this dream of complete self-sufficiency in the final two lines, where Roosevelt the stone "lets the marriage bed fall" and, finally, self-destructs in order to prove himself invincible, by leaping into the water to drown the man who is trying to rob him. The psychic values of Roosevelt, and their failure, are part of history's legacy to the presidency in the sixties; for Bly, the president's desire to be feared by other countries ("I ate the Cubans with a straw, and Lenin dreamt of *me* every night") is a major cause of the Vietnam War.

Bly's portrayal of Kennedy is less obvious than that of the first two presidents. Kennedy is imaged as "a stream of water falling," a pure force of nature that flows around problems and carries them "with me to the valley." Kennedy dreams of a presidency of pure style, of a landscape of manageable problems, of the triumph of the managerial-scientific style that characterized the third great national effort of the sixties, the space program to reach the moon. For Bly, Kennedy believed that government could succeed by enlisting "the best and the brightest" to manage and solve problems; but the flaw in this philos-

ophy is that it ignores the existence of evil, the intractable knot at
the center of human personality that can only be undone by individual effort and hard work. Thus Bly has Kennedy dream of the glory
of "the old life, before it was ruined by the Church," and desire to
ascend and "fall forever, / Missing the earth entirely." This final image, an ironic association through the resurrection/ascension image of
Kennedy and Christ, really a mocking of managerial man as Christ,
was used again by Bly, much more forcefully, in the final image of
"The Teeth Mother Naked at Last." There the space program mentality of man's triumph through technology is parodied through the image of driving cars to the stars, as a superficial, external journey that
always ends with a realization that man's real exploration must be inward, through the depths of his own personality, his soul. Kennedy's
personal attractiveness is a function of his superficiality, his refusal to
believe in the intractable problems of human nature. In "Listening to
President Kennedy Lie about the Cuban Invasion" Bly portrays Kennedy as superficial in his refusal to acknowledge the dark side of life,
both personal and political, of the "darkness in the fences of the
body," of government lying to the people. For Bly, Kennedy's lie on
television dispelled much more than the personal idealism he had
brought to the presidency. The lie dispelled for both Kennedy and
the nation the illusion of a world comprehensible to reason alone, a
world where all problems could be resolved by a clever management
style coupled with good will, a world without evil, without its
shadow side. It was this world that the pragmatic American psyche
had always longed for, and which it had been promised by Kennedy.

"The Vietnam War"

Section 3 of *Light* is titled "The Vietnam War." Its theme is the
complex relationship between the inward, psychological life of the nation and its external, political life, as exposed by its participation in
the Vietnam war. Bly invokes history to suggest that the causes of
the war, and especially of what seemed in the sixties to be the especially barbarous nature of the war, were more psychological than political, going back to a racist mentality manifest in America from its
very beginning.[20] From the Puritans' attitude toward the Indians as
"darkness" and evil in "At a March against the Vietnam War" to
their ancestors' tacit approval of the slave trade in "Hearing Men
Shout at Night on MacDougal Street," from the pioneers' belief in a

manifest destiny that sanctioned their "longings to kill" Indians in "As the Asian War Begins" to America's long history of "Hatred of Men with Black Hair," Bly traces the history of the willingness of Americans to act more barbarously toward enemies not of the Caucasian race. He links this to the vigorous American repression of the shadow side of the national psyche, and to a concomitant psychodynamic, the scapegoat phenomenon. In this dynamic the ego first dissociates itself from its alter ego, the shadow it has repressed, and then projects it outward, onto some person or group. The ego then hates this scapegoat person all the more for symbolizing the part of the psyche which the ego unconsciously fears and hates, which it calls evil. Perhaps the most straightforward linkage of these concepts occurs in Bly's antiwar play, "The Satisfaction of Vietnam," where one character explains: "If a man can't see his shadow, then he's longing for death, he is ready for death, death enters the space between a man and his shadow."[21] Similarly, in "At a March against the Vietnam War," Bly explains the nation's self-abasement in the Vietnam War, its turning its back on the traditional American values of liberty and human rights. Bly presents it as the fulfillment of a psychological compulsion, an immersion in darkness which the nation desires because it compensates for the nation's long history of repression of its dark side, as symbolized by its repression of races of color. Satisfying this compulsion brings relief: "We long to abase ourselves / We make war / Like a man anointing himself." Our nation's psyche is so twisted that satisfaction comes from a perverse act, one harmful to the national soul. Of course, not all critics agree with Bly's analysis, or with his use of it in poetry. Those with a political orientation, especially, see Bly's dependence on psychology as wrong, as bad politics. Todd Gitlin calls it a "reversion to a vulgar Freudianism, a shallow idea that makes for shallow poetry."[22]

Bly amplifies on the psychohistorical causes of the war by describing their contemporary manifestations in the men of the government who prosecute the war. In "Asian Peace Offers Rejected without Publication" Bly images Secretary of State Rusk and his aides as caught in the most extreme of contradictions, on the one hand "Talking of Teilhard de Chardin," the humanist theologian who wrote of mankind's evolving toward a glorious future, and on the other hand rejecting peace offers and "longing" to keep playing war games. Bly calls them "bombs" rather than men, and he means that they are so caught up in a psychological compulsion that they have lost their human imagination and free will; they are capable of exploding, but not of feeling the contradiction. Bly's image for this state of mind is that these government executives are under the spell of old movie fantasies, imagining themselves in a World War II movie, as pilots fighting a just war. The extreme split between inward and outward worlds that characterizes their behavior reveals itself in their choice of entertainment. After the bombing run these State Department John Waynes "start the projector, and show the movie about the mad professor," unaware that it reflects their own faustian mentality.

But the poem's second half refutes their attitude by taking up what is the most important theme of this section of the book, the effect of the war on the inward life of the nation and of the individual. For Bly, the overlooked victim of the Vietnam War was the American soul, "Lost angels huddled on a night branch!" The war's greatest loss was "something inside us / like a ghost train in The Rockies / about to be buried in snow." Again the poet uses a variation on his major symbol of snow to announce the true threat: an avalanche that obliterates the soul, rather than a gentle snowfall that covers and nourishes it, is his image for the disastrous effect of the war. The "long hoot" of this soul about to be buried is a cry of the heart that should awaken the head to wisdom, alerting "the owl in the Douglas fir."

But the most extensive statement of the profound effect of the war on the inward life occurs in the final poem of section 3, "Driving through Minnesota during the Hanoi Bombings." The poem begins with Bly driving through the countryside amid signs of nature's renewal in the lakes and "new grass." He thinks about incidents of Americans torturing Vietnamese, shooting them from helicopters, killing them to put them out of the misery Americans have inflicted. For the poet these "instants become crystals" in the psyche, out of the reach of seasonal time and natural renewal, "Particles / which the grass cannot dissolve."[23] In the psychic life events may be ever-present, both in cause and in effect. They cannot be eradicated by political, external acts because they are psychological, inward conditions of the soul. This is why Americans are also victims of the war, even though it occurs in South Vietnam and now Hanoi: "Our own gaiety / Will end up / in Asia." For Bly the escalation of the war into North Vietnam with the bombing of Hanoi was symbolic of America's psychological perturbation, caused by the guilt over both the racist causes and the barbaric means of the war: "We were the ones we intended to bomb!" Bly introduces the psychoreligious concept of atonement as the only solution to the kind of war being fought in Vietnam. It is not merely that the war is immoral, but also that the causes are much more psychological than political, which makes atonement the only kind of solution possible to the real dangers to America posed by the Vietnam War. As in the conclusion of "At a March Against the Vietnam War," so here Bly uses the religious imagery ironically. On the one hand, he expresses his bitterness toward the bombings by using "atone" to describe ironically America's rationale that bombings are less personal acts of war than shooting people from helicopters; on the other hand, Bly uses the word seriously to suggest that through the bombings we are psychologically acting out our guilt and therefore our desire for atonement, and thus admitting subconsciously that the true causes of the war are psychological and not political, inward and not outward. Thus it is that the poem is a fitting conclusion to both the inward and outward struggle of the Vietnam War.

"In Praise of Grief"

One of the most significant changes Bly made between the American and British editions of *Light* involved a shift of emphasis regarding section 4. Apparently he felt that in the American arrangement section 4, titled "In Praise of Grief," struck a tone more appropriate to unmitigated despair than to redemptive despair. The epigraphs to sections 4 and 5, especially the latter, emphasize the inconsolable nature of the grief caused by the conflict between the inner life and the outer worlds of business, government, and war presented in sections 1 through 3. But in many ways the poems themselves reach for the vision of redemption and resurrection just glimpsed on the far side of the vale of tears where inner and outer worlds conflict. Bly's changes in the British edition signal his final intentions for the book. He concludes section 4 with the hopeful poem "Looking into a Face," and perhaps more importantly moves "The Fire of Despair Has Been Our Saviour" from the end to the middle, thus subduing its fatalistic and, by Bly's own admission (*T*, 124), flawed final image of "Not finding the road, we are slowly pulled down." Thus Bly has tried in the British edition to redirect the reader's attention to his book's overall emphasis on the positive aspects of the inward life. In this case his

changes argue for a rereading of the final two parts of *Light,* a shift
of emphasis from melancholy to the praise of grief in section 4, and
from sadness to joy in section 5.

The religious imagery Bly used at the conclusion of section 3 plays
a more prominent role in sections 4 and 5. The concept of atonement,
used in section 3, is invoked by Bly to entangle both traditional religion and depth psychology. In section 4 the paradox of the title, "In
Praise of Grief," is best understood in similar psychoreligious terms.
In seven poems Bly builds a network of psychoreligious imagery that
serves as a foundation for the joyful hope of section 5. Bly finds in
this entangling of the religious and the psychological not only a
strengthened resolve to look beyond the conflict of the two worlds,
but also a justification for the validity of his belief in the archetypal
patterns of depth psychology. That the Judaeo-Christian myth of glory,
ruin, and restoration corresponds to Bly's hope of rising from grief
into "a body / not yet born" only proves the universality of the emotion.

Thus, although the season of section 4 is autumn, and the subject
is grief, with funerals beginning and ending the section, still the tone
is not the unredeemed "Melancholia" that the initial poem's title
might suggest. Indeed, Bly has spoken of funerals as occasions notable for the many "perceptions coming in from the unconscious" (*T,*
125). And the idea of a "Saviour" figures prominently in several of
the poems: "A Home in Dark Grass" and "The Fire of Despair Has
Been Our Saviour." In the latter, in the image of "O holy trees, re-
joicing ruin of leaves," Bly seems to invoke the ancient concept of the
felix culpa, the fortunate fall, a paradoxical theme that appears in the
Mass of Holy Saturday, before Easter Sunday. There the church
praises the Fall of Adam in the Garden of Eden because, paradoxically, the original sin brought to man a great reward, his redeemer
Jesus Christ. Bly, of course, does not mean this to be taken in nar-
rowly Christian terms, as an argument for avoiding grief by ignoring
the conflict between inner and outer worlds and looking beyond to
the other world of heaven. Indeed, a major source of grief in "Melancholia" is the failure of organized religion to nourish its followers by
convincing them of a life after death; attending a funeral of a friend,
Bly enters "A cathedral: I see / Starving men, weakened, leaning /
on their knees." And Bly declares flatly in "Turning Away From Lies,"
that "Christ did not come to redeem our sins," and, most importantly, that "The two worlds are both in this world." But imagery

such as "The wind rises / the water is born, / Spreading white tomb-clothes on a rocky shore," from "A Home in Dark Grass," emphasizes Bly's reasons for praising grief, the hope of resurrection, in a natural imagery subtly freighted with a whisper of Christianity's argument that it is indeed a fortunate fall that leads to a resurrection.

The section's final poem, "Looking at Some Flowers," reinforces this interpretation. It presents four images of natural things at a funeral that seem to belong to two worlds simultaneously, four images of liminality. The poem has light, flowers, and even the casket "not knowing which world it is in." These elements of nature, in straddling two worlds, underscore life's fundamental action as continual evolution from one stage to the next, from one world to another. Thus they suggest a hopeful, psychoreligious association between evolution and resurrection, and give support to Bly's argument for praising grief.

"A Body Not Yet Born"

The final section of the American edition of *Light* is titled "A Body Not Yet Born." The British edition's change of titles, to "The Two Worlds," and especially its corresponding change of epigraphs, emphasizes hope. Just as inward conflicts caused the sociopolitical problems of the first three sections of poetry, so too can inward solutions help to redeem those imperfections so manifest in the outward worlds of business, government and war.

Section 5 is characterized by a hopeful, even celebratory, poetry of transformation and resurrection. There are reminders of the more somber moods of the earlier sections, most evident in "Hurrying Away from the Earth" and "Riderless Horses." But the dominant mood is represented not only by the opening poem, "Looking Into a Face," but also by "A Journey with Women," "Moving Inward at Last," "Evolution from the Fish," and "Wanting to Experience All Things." The concluding poem, "When the Dumb Speak," attempts to harmonize the two moods in a final, apocalyptic dream-vision of a world ruled by the psychoreligious laws of inwardness.

The first poem, "Looking into a Face," is a powerful statement in psychoreligious terms of Bly's belief in the possibility of new life. It is a poem that looks forward in important ways to his next major book, *Sleepers Joining Hands,* with its emphasis on inwardness, intimacy, and the private poetic voice. The poem's theme, a development

from the previous "Looking at Some Flowers," is that there is a
higher state of being that appears in glimpses, like "a light around
the body," toward which mankind is developing. The poet knows
this state sometimes through intimate conversation with another, instants when man's collective evolutionary history and its instinctual
urge toward further life energizes him, reminding him of ancient
"surfs of the body, / Bringing fish up near the sun, / And stiffening
the backbones of the sea!" Through conversation with another individual the poet joins in communion with all of the human race, past
and present, so that the intimate relationship of two people becomes
the basis for the widest possible collective act, participation in the
collective unconscious, sharing in the furtherance of the race.

Bly uses his psychoreligious imagery to present his glimpse of
mankind's essential freedom and collective future. Teleology, the idea
that human personality is formed to some extent by the pull of unconscious goals, and thus is not (as Freud would have it) wholly de-
termined by early childhood and the past, is an important part of
Jung's optimistic vision of even the disturbances which occur in the
evolutionary human psyche, as it is of Teilhard de Chardin's philosophy. Bly declares, "I have risen to a body / Not yet born, / Existing
like a light around the body." Bly's sense that man is destined for a
higher stage of evolution is imaged here as a resurrection into a new
form, one "not yet born," that is, not yet incorporated so completely
into the natural cycle that it reproduces itself. This new body is to
the old one as the aura of moonlight is to that cold, dark rock itself:
an external light source that seems to pull along, to lead out, the object within. Thus the light is like a goal that calls forth the body to
move toward it, to aspire to become "the light around the body."
Both image and theme link Bly's, like Jung's, conceptualization of
the teleology of the human psyche with that of the evolution of the
human brain, as described in Bly's essay "The Three Brains."

Several earlier poems in *Light* presented Bly's belief that such "instants," glimpses of the future stages of evolution are important moments for the race. In "Driving through Minnesota during the Hanoi
Bombings" Bly had spoken of the permanent damage to our evolutionary psyche, instants which could not be easily outgrown through
the normal processes of nature, caused by the experiences of the Vietnam war: "These instants become crystals, / Particles / The grass cannot dissolve." Throughout section 4, but especially in "The Fire of
Despair Has Been our Saviour," Bly cited similar moments in human

evolutionary history when, under extreme duress, great leaps forward had been made, "instants / Finally leading out of the snowbound valley!" Here, in "Looking into a Face," the surge of instinctual energy pushing the poet into the "light around the body" is just such an instant of personal breakthrough, presaging hope for his own and mankind's collective future. Thus its selection for the title of the entire book is an important indication that Bly always perceived the inward, psychological life to be ultimately stronger and more important for mankind than the external, political life of a particular historical moment. The inward life is more than a refuge and an escape from the world; for Bly it is the fundamental basis for the life of the world.

"A Journey with Women" may be understood as the antithesis of the masculine ego's attack on mother consciousness and its associated psychic values, delivered earlier in "The Busy Man Speaks." Like the poem before it, "The Hermit," this is a poem about a dream, about dreaming itself, which Bly images here as taking a journey into another part of our psyche. The first three stanzas image three ways of going into the dream state. It begins with the poet rocking to sleep, either through ordinary drifting off or perhaps through making love. In either case, the passage is a transformation, back to an earlier stage of human evolution, in which the dead of mankind's evolutionary past merely "sleep in jars," archetypes of collective human wisdom waiting for the right moment to arise and teach the dreamer their wisdom. The poem's turtle imagery conveys the sense of ancient memory combined with wisdom, especially when the world's many myths of the turtle as the wise foundation of the planet Earth itself are recalled. The mothers, the "women" of the title, are invoked in stanza 2 in the form of the moon, the "white goddess" of myth who lights man's way down the "tunnels" of sleep leading to the "sea" of dreams and the unconscious life. The previous poem, "The Hermit," had used a similar image of the archetypal wise man pointing the way to "sail on into the tunnels of joyful death," the happy death in which ego-consciousness gives way to the dream state. In stanza 3 the poet, deep in sleep, sees himself as "Waking" into the wisdom of a dream, one in which the flying tortoise (a common figure in African legends) carries the dreamer farther and farther from the present society of patriarchal ego-consciousness, here imaged appropriately as the heavily industrialized former garden state of "New Jersey." The poem's final stanza finds the poet completely transformed into another state of consciousness. Literally, he describes the common feeling people have just before they start to awaken. Figuratively, he describes the dreamer as a moon, a transparency "pulling / In the starlight . . . Full of moonlight," transformed almost wholly from a solid object into that "light around the body," that next, higher stage of evolution imaged in the first poem of this section.

"Moving Inward at Last," the next poem, presents new images for these magical moments of transformation in the inward life. The poem begins with a failed sacrifice, "the dying bull" whose blood is not felt "inside the mountain." The bull symbolizes not only the ineffectual formalistic sacrifices of organized religion, but also the failure of the masculine ego to succeed without its anima. Both are examples of futile attempts to evolve while ignoring, or repressing, the feminine side of the psyche. But inside the mountain of consciousness is a shaman spirit who tends a fire, surrounded by remnants of successful evolutions of the masculine, such as "antlers, bits of oak bark." At a certain instant, "When the smoke touches the roof of the cave" and an unbearable temperature is reached, both inward and outward transformations occur: leaves become flame, air turns to water, the mountains "alter and become the sea" of the unconscious, inward life. The pun on "altar" subtly underscores the difference between the successful transformation from within and the failure of the formal religious sacrifice of the bull, a ritual of grandiose external symbolism unaccompanied by inward transformation.

"Evolution from the Fish" unites the images of transformation and resurrection in a playful, joyful poem about making love. The poem's extended comparison is between two people making love and their awakening to the history and instinctual fervor of the evolutionary spirit within. The poet begins by calling himself "This grandson of fishes . . . This nephew of snails." The section's central image of light as signifying a higher evolutionary stage is prominent. The poet's brain "throws off light" under his skull's "marble," and the psyche's teleological imperative is satisfied, for in making love Bly declares "he is moving toward his own life." In the second and final stanza, Bly associates new human life with nature's own processes, in the common smell of "a new child! / Like new grass!" The physical forces are imbued with spiritual significance as well, as Bly suggests by imaging the courtship stage as "the spirit moving around them." The ecstasy of sexual climax is similarly associated with nature's evolutionary processes, perhaps even with Christ's resurrection, in this image: "In the dark we blaze up, drawing pictures / Of spiny fish, we throw off the white stones!" The poem concludes by giving testimony to the power of the experience as a spiritual as well as physical phenomenon. In the image of a fire "passing up through the soles of my feet" there is, again through a gentle pun, an implication of the spirit, the soul itself, in the evolution this poem describes.

In "Wanting to Experience All Things" Bly underscores his enduring belief in the inward road by criticizing one of the fundamental tenets of the sixties, the primacy of experience. He compares, unfavorably, the romantic, outward-directed emotion to the psychological, inward motion. He begins with two images of the human condition, of mankind's blindness to the true delights of his existence and of human mortality, "bones, sticking from the cool earth." Against this background, the romantic tries to escape, leaping "Almost up to the sky," only to be pulled "back into the darkness." This failure, and consequent recognition of mankind's blindness, prepares for an inspiration from within. In an image very much like one at the conclusion of "Sleepers Joining Hands," Bly sees the panther of the unconscious asserting its power: "But a paw / Comes out of the dark / To light the road." The inward experience which the unconscious asserts is much more powerful than anything the romantic could imagine. The poet is "flying," no longer leaping futilely toward the sky. And the experience he has is not of the external world's "cherry trees," but of his inward and collective self: "I follow my own fiery traces through the night!"

Light's final poem, "When the Dumb Speak," conjoins the book's two major themes of inwardness and the intractability of the external world.

> There is a joyful night in which we lose
> Everything, and drift
> Like a radish
> Rising and falling, and the ocean
> At last throws us into the ocean,
> And on the water we are sinking
> As if floating on darkness.
> The body raging
> And driving itself, disappearing in smoke,
> Walks in large cities late at night,
> Or reading the Bible in Christian Science windows,
> Or reading a history of Bougainville.
> Then the images appear:

> Images of death,
> Images of the body shaken in the grave,
> And the graves filled with seawater;
> Fires in the sea,
> The ships smoldering like bodies,
> Images of wasted life,
> Life lost, imagination ruined,
> The house fallen,
> The gold sticks broken,
> Then shall the talkative be silent,
> And the dumb shall speak.

This poem presents a dream-vision of "a joyful night" in which, para-doxically, a loss shall become a gain, a night when "the dumb shall speak." The prevalence of paradox and biblical language in this poem is reinforced by the allusion in the title to the prophecy of Isaiah 35.6. This prophecy is about the miracles that will accompany the triumphant second coming of the Saviour, "and the tongue of the dumb shall sing," in a verse known to many through its inclusion in Handel's *Messiah*. Paradox and biblical language are important psy-chological and religious elements in Bly's attempt to resolve the con-flict between "the two worlds" presented at the book's beginning by invoking a final vision of a perfectly harmonized world to come, a world of the inner spirit. The poem begins by describing the paradox of going to sleep, of sinking into unconsciousness yet "floating on darkness." After seven lines the poet images the intellect's frustration that must precede its submission to the joyful descent into sleep. In "the body raging / And driving itself" Bly images the body of the ego-consciousness roaring its motor in an inevitably futile attempt to solve the conflicts and to think through the paradoxes the sociopoliti-cal world presents, such as "the Bible in Christian Science windows," or "a history of Bougainville," that war-ravaged natural paradise. After the mind has spun itself out, "Then the images appear," of an apocalypse in which "Life lost, imagination ruined" shall occur and, paradoxically, prepare for a new order, ruled by the laws of the har-monized soul achieved through the pursuit of inwardness. After the spell of patriarchal domination of consciousness is broken, compared by Bly to the archetypal denouements of a Greek tragedy or a fairy tale in the lines "The house fallen, / The gold sticks broken," then shall the new order appear, "Then shall the talkative be silent, / And the dumb shall speak." Though this poem is primarily about a transformation of consciousness within the individual, brought on by the movement from waking to dreaming, there is still a sense of its application to the external world. The poem presents an apocalyptic vision which Bly images again in much more elaborate fashion in his next book, in the long poem "The Teeth Mother Naked at Last." Here he concludes the psychoreligious imagery that infuses the last two sections of *Light* as the Bible itself does, with the destruction of the external world as man knows it in preparation for the rule of the spiritual. The political laments that began *Light* have given way to eschatological prophesies, as they must in a vision that believes that "many of the events that create our foreign relations and our domestic relations come from more or less hidden impulses in the American psyche" (*F*, 10), that inwardness precedes political life. Bly's conclusion demonstrates that in *Light* he is writing not only a book of political poetry, but also a book challenging the very way in which most people ordinarily think about politics in relation to their lives.

Chapter Four
The Poetry of Psychospiritual Myth: *Sleepers Joining Hands*

To move from *The Light Around the Body* to *Sleepers Joining Hands* is to measure the distance between the sixties and the seventies in America, both for the country and for Robert Bly. This transition is expressed succinctly at the conclusion of Bly's 1969 poem "The Teeth Mother Naked at Last," in the juxtaposition of the macrocosmic image of the Teeth Mother threatening civilization itself with the microcosmic image of the individual being tortured by his own psychospiritual sins. The movement from concern with external events, such as the Vietnam War or the space race, which characterized the sixties, capitulates in the seventies to a concern with inward events, even if for many people this means only the egotistical wants, needs, and desires of what has been characterized as a "me" generation. For Bly himself, *Sleepers* represents a turning away from a poetry dominated by a public persona addressing public issues, and a turning toward a poetry much more personal and introspective than even that presented in his first book, *Silence*. It is as though after all the public activity of the mid and late sixties, Bly's imagination began a compensatory program of self-examination, an effort to image forth and thereby understand the hidden conflicts of a successful and public figure whose earliest and strongest commitment was to the pursuit of the inward road. *Sleepers,* then, represents a hail and farewell to the zeitgeist of a decade.

Robert Bly's third major book is composed of three different parts, representing a far broader range of writing than either *Silence* or *Light*. Part 1, the longest, consists of ten short poems, all previously published in magazines, and the long antiwar poem, "The Teeth Mother Naked at Last," which was published as a separate book[1] three years before. "The Teeth Mother" had gained notoriety through its dramatic presentation, and even on-the-spot composition,[2] at Bly's many readings during the Vietnam period; indeed, Joyce Carol Oates called it "the finest poem to have grown out of the antiwar movement."[3] Part 2 of *Sleepers* is a twenty-two-page essay describing the cross-cultural, archetypal myth of the Great Mother, which figures prominently in the poetry of parts 1 and 3. Part 3 is a fifteen-page selection from what Bly says is a much longer and still unfinished poem of spiritual autobiography, "Sleepers Joining Hands." This is the most ambitious of Bly's poems to date; the astute critic Charles Molesworth has judged "Sleepers" as worthy of "comparison to the best of contemporary poetry."[4]

Although such a book is clearly a collection of diverse materials, the book's arrangement traces a recognizable development. The book opens on a note of private joy, moves through the personal and social desolation symbolized by the psychic ruin of Vietnam, and concludes with a triumphant reaffirmation, a restoration of hope for both the individual and the human community. Nevertheless, the differences between the book's parts, especially between part 1 and parts 2 and 3, often seem greater than the similarities. The reader senses that the book represents a transition in Bly's development, reflecting at least two different periods of his career, and two different aspects of his poetic imagination.

Part 1 of *Sleepers* presents two basic groupings of poems: those about politics and those about human evolutionary psychology. The political group consists of poems similar to those in Bly's previous book, *Light*. In this group belong all the poems in the second half of part 1 of *Sleepers*, from "Hair" to "The Teeth Mother Naked at Last." The second group includes poems celebrating, albeit in an understated way, the larger process of evolutionary psychology (both individual and collective). Even a crisis of psychic blockage and despair can be seen as having a dual nature, both negative and positive, and thus as a potential opportunity to be assimilated and integrated into a personality (and its poetry) whose central impulse is to evolve toward the achievement of a higher state of individuation, of selfhood. Poems in this group comprise those of the first half of part 1, from "Six Winter Privacy Poems" to "In a Mountain Cabin in Norway."

In part 1, then, Bly presents five poems dealing with the larger process of psychic evolution. He then follows with the poems cataloging the despair of the current political and cultural condition, in six poems describing a rising curve of intensity that peaks with the apocalyptic "The Teeth Mother Naked at Last." Thus part 1 of the book moves from hope to a psychic crisis of personal and collective despair.

The hopeful theme of human psychospiritual growth in the first half of part 1, the theme that provides the counterpoint to the vision of desolation symbolized by Vietnam in the second half, is evident in three poems about the joys of exploring the private, inward life, "Six Winter Privacy Poems," "Shack Poem," and "In a Mountain Cabin in Norway." Especially the first, which one critic praised as "among Bly's best work,"[5] expresses the joy of private exploration of the psyche, the rewards of inward discovery in "I can't tell if this joy / is from the body, or the soul, or a third place." The last stanza uses Bly's most enduring image, the snow, to establish the psychospiritual landscape, the mood, that accompanies the ecstatic discoveries possible to the explorer of the inward life: "When I woke, the new snow had fallen. / I am alone, yet someone else is with me, / drinking coffee, looking out at the snow."

Another interesting poem from the first half of part 1 is "Water Under the Earth," which in many ways looks forward to the book's final, title poem. For instance, the title's image of the nourishing water of the unconscious that lies beneath the visible earth of conscious existence is central to Bly's use of the story of Jonah's voyage in the belly of the whale, which in "Sleepers" symbolizes the process by which humans first doubt, then discover and are reborn into, a faith in the powers of the unconscious as well as the conscious levels of their existence. This final image of "Water Under the Earth," of the newborn man united with both the past in the "underground rivers," and the future through "his children," is nearly identical to Bly's later image of "sleepers joining hands," of a human community united through its collective unconscious and its common evolutionary goals. Further, this poem introduces many of the images from nature that Bly develops throughout the book into symbols of aspects of psychic life. The stag's antlers, the owl, the badger, the leopard, the bull, the white horse, the willow, underground rivers—all these images of the first half of part 1 reappear in other poems in the book, especially in part 3's long poem "Sleepers Joining Hands."

The poems of the second half of part 1 are not spoken in the private voice used for those in the first half, but instead are like the political poems of *Light*. They express the psychic division and antagonism that characterizes the Vietnam period of American history by establishing a linkage between categories usually thought of as separate—

the personality, the economy, the environment, history. Even more than the poems in *Light,* these depend heavily on rhetorical flourish and an exaggerated stridency of voice to project the poet's persona of public scourge. This extreme shift in voice between the first half and the second half of part 1 is evident in many ways. For instance, Bly's reworking of Whitman's humble yet cosmic imagery in such lines as "There is a consciousness hovering under the mind's feet, advanced civilizations under the footsole," which concludes "Water Under the Earth," is in striking contrast to the Ginsberg-like howling voice that addresses "you United States" just five poems later, at the opening of the poem "Conditions of the Working Class: 1970." Even the poems of this section which reach for the inward emotions, such as the "sadness" of "Calling to the Badger" or the mordant irony of "Pilgrim Fish Heads," have an almost exclusively public tone about them. They are, finally, utterances attempting to speak for the collective "we" about the psychopolitical sins of America's collective heritage.

"The Teeth Mother Naked at Last": A Reading

The major poem of part 1, and perhaps the best postmodern war poem in American literature, is "The Teeth Mother Naked at Last." As Bly's involvement with the antiwar movement grew through the sixties, as the war itself intensified, he responded to the challenge by developing what might be described as a poetics of apocalypse. There are two new elements of this poetics introduced in "The Teeth Mother." The first is the expression in both theme and style of Bly's increasing belief that in times of extreme partisan politics the poet's first duty is to serve as the defender of the integrity of the language itself by exposing its politicization and subversion. The second new element of Bly's poetics here is his overt use, in passages crucial to the poem's success, of the Jungian model of the psyche, especially Jung's concept of a collective unconscious that expresses itself through such archetypal symbols as the Teeth Mother. Bly uses such symbols to present the poet's revelations in what is potentially their most dramatic and universal form.

A major problem facing any political poet of the Vietnam period was to resuscitate the language itself from the stultifying effect of unrelenting media exposure. After seven years of nightly newscasts and morning newspapers, the war had come to be understood by the American public mainly in the terms used by the media to "cover"

it, which were often the same terms as those used by the government
and the Pentagon to defend it. Bly felt that the vital American language had become sanitized and weakened by these usages, drained
of energy either from the government's intentional laundering of the
language's inherent political associations, or from the media's repetition of the same terms day in and day out, or from the various speak-
ers' blatant lack of knowledge of the war-reality they professed to be
describing. The languages of newsspeak, Defense Department bureau-
cratese, etc., all dulled the reader's critical awareness, just as the infa-
mous "body counts" on the nightly news blurred the reality of
America's lack of success in the war.

Bly's strategy in "The Teeth Mother" is not to ignore or circum-
vent this fundamental problem of the subversion of language, but to
confront and expose it: to turn the media-enervated language back on
itself, to enable the self-correcting laws of language to work, by high-
lighting and juxtaposing the language's many corrupted wartime
guises. In recognizing the incongruity of language with fact, or of
one language-version with another, the reader is forced to become
aware not only of instances of lies and deceptions, but more importantly of the fundamental dislocation of sensibility this co-opting and
corrupting of language has caused in the American psyche.

Bly declares this corruption of language as a major theme early in
his poem: "The ministers lie, the professors lie, the television lies,
the priests lie. . . . / These lies mean that the country wants to die"
(*S*, 21). And he amplifies this theme by sprinkling throughout the
poem fragments of language *qua* language, as emblems of various
class, sexual, and racial interests rather than of a disinterested medium of honest, direct communication between people. For example,
Bly quotes President Lyndon Johnson in this revealing juxtaposition
of languages:

> *"Let us not be deterred from our task by the voices*
>   *of dissent. . . ."*
> The whines of the jets
> pierce like a long needle.
> As soon as the President finishes his press
> conference, black wings carry off the words,
> bits of flesh still clinging to them.
>   (*S*, 20–21)

Similarly, the language of statistics and numbers associated by Bly with an overbearing masculine consciousness, the antithesis of mother consciousness, is pervasive throughout the poem's first section. After describing an air strike in terms of a fragmented technological jargon, such as "wings with eight hundred rivets" and "Engines burning a thousand gallons of gasoline a minute," Bly confronts the inherent deception in this techno-militarist jargon, its inference that only machines are involved in the daily air strikes that characterized the war. Bly applies a machine-word to a human being in this outrageously incongruous context:

> Artillery shells explode. Napalm cannisters
> roll end over end.
> 800 steel pellets fly through vegetable walls.
> The six-hour infant puts his fist instinctively
> to his eyes to keep out the light.
> But the room explodes,
> the children explode.
> Blood leaps on the vegetable walls.
>
> (*S*, 19)

This shocking image of children exploding exposes the techno-militarist jargon as just as subversive of America's proclaimed humanitarian interests as the stratofortress. Bly thus attempts to show how the emotional coldness and distance inherent in the abstraction of a scientific and technological language can induce a de facto capitulation of responsibility that leads to atrocities such as carpet bombing and Hiroshima.

Bly's strategy of exposing the state's co-opting of language, and thereby suggesting how the politics of language is evident in all forms of its use (even in Bly's own poetry), is made most explicit in this passage from the beginning of section 3: "this is what it's like to bomb huts (afterwards described as 'structures') / this is what it's like to kill marginal farmers (afterwards described as 'Communists')" In an interview Bly explained his own understanding of the possibilities and dangers of a poet's using this technique of incorporating a collage of different kinds of language, with very different relationships to truth and vitality, in his poem. Bly cites the above passage as an example of the most obvious kind of lying through word selection, noting "in that line you can see that the technocrats have withdrawn energy from the word 'structures' in order to tell lies about what they are doing." Bly goes on to cite the less obvious, though more fundamental and dangerous, problem for society as well as its poets—that of trying to communicate truth with a language that has been polluted by so many intentionally and unintentionally devious language tricks. The poet warns that "you have to be aware of who is withdrawing energy from a word before you put it into a poem, otherwise it'll withdraw energy from your poem. Since so many words have had their energy corrupted, it's very difficult to write poetry" (T, 229).

The poetic structure of "The Teeth Mother" balances Bly's cataloging of examples of America's polluted and politicized language by setting it against a relatively formal poetic design, and both language examples and design gain by the interaction. The poem is greatly strengthened at the rhetorical level by the use of a very long line, one especially suited to the speaker's public and oratorical voice. Bly uses a structure of seven numbered sections, each of which is separated by asterisks; this structure of many formal divisions, spread over nine pages, supports the speaker/performer's radical and dramatic shifts of tone and subject in his catalogs and declamations.[6]

The second new element of Bly's poetics in "The Teeth Mother" is his overt use of the Jungian model of the psyche, specifically, the archetypal Teeth Mother, to dramatize his message. As in Light, Bly argues that the war was best understood as an effect, a symbolic act, caused by a conflict in the individual's and the nation's collective life. The war did not create trouble for America; rather, it exposed a trouble that already existed in the American psyche. As Bly explained, "an event like the Vietnam war can be traced to 'imperialism' and financial manipulations. But the poems on the war . . . tried to give inward reasons for that war" (T, 154–55). But the aspect of Bly's poetic strategy original to "The Teeth Mother" is the final apocalyptic image of the Teeth Mother. The Teeth Mother appears at the climax of the poem, in a passage whose dramatic import is felt by the reader mainly because of its position at the natural climax of the poem, aided by whatever sound and mask effects with which the performing poet might embellish it. Bly would also justify such an archetypal symbol as having "links . . . to the biological evolutionary part of the mind" (T, 7).[7] But its full meaning may be unclear to the reader, because the Teeth Mother symbol is mythic and archetypal, rather than historical, and therefore unfamiliar at the conscious level to most Americans. Further, the symbol has not been introduced previously, let alone built up, in the poem. In defense of Bly's strategy, however, Jung might be cited: "one encounters projections, one does not make them";[8] they always emanate from the unconscious, to surprise the conscious mind, like a good or bad dream.

Bly's explanatory essay immediately following the poem describes the archetype of mother consciousness as consisting of four parts, symbolized by four faces: Good Mother—Death Mother, and Ecstatic Mother—Teeth Mother. The Teeth Mother symbolizes the "dismembering of the psyche" (*S*, 41), and her opposite symbolizes the Muse, who joyfully renews the psyche with song and poetry. These two opposites are revealed at the poem's climactic moment, "naked at last," symbols of the choice everyone must make in his psychic life. Bly means it to be a moment of revelation of an important truth about the American national psyche evoked by the Vietnam War: Americans are killing others because they are not psychically whole themselves; they have repressed their soulful feminine consciousness, and now the return of the repressed takes a form that threatens the nation with psychic disintegration. This is Bly's ultimate argument for America's perceiving the political fact of the Vietnam War as both a personal and a political crisis, the ultimate expression of his poetics of apocalypse: "the waters underneath part: in one ocean luminous globes float up (in them hairy and ecstatic men—) / in the other, the teeth mother, naked at last" (*S*, 26). The choice is offered between the Ecstatic Mother and the Teeth Mother. The former offers a vision of a world populated by men whose hairiness, as in *Hair,* the popular play/film of the late sixties, signifies acceptance and assimilation of their feminine aspect. The latter offers a threatening vision of social and psychic disintegration, one which the previous parts of the poem have already hinted at in describing the apocalypse of America's Vietnam.

Although the appearance of the Teeth Mother is the poem's dramatic climax, the imagery of the poem's coda, the final seven lines, is more important in tying together the whole work and relating it to Bly's enduring poetic theme of man's inward, psychospiritual journey. These last lines image the contrast between the most extravagant outward American technological triumph of the sixties, rocketing a man (along with a car) to the Moon, and Vietnam, that decade's gravest American failure. The final image reaffirms the necessity of triumphant journeys through inward space, by emphasizing that no matter how far away the rockets fly or the cars drive, they cannot escape, let alone heal, man's inward psychospiritual conflicts. In America's case it is the conflicted, mother-denying Protestant heritage that, in Bly's vision, is responsible for Vietnam and the eruption of the long-re-pressed Teeth Mother in the American psyche. The image of the space explorer returning to earth in a capsule of a "drop of sweat" is a strik-ing allusion to perhaps the best known visual image of space travel in the sixties, the foetus of the reborn space traveler at the conclusion of the film *2001: A Space Odyssey*. Like a whip-lash cracking, this coda abruptly returns the reader to awareness that inward success or failure always takes precedence over achievement in the external world.

Thus Bly's poetic strategy in "The Teeth Mother" is based not only on reclaiming the language, but also on redefining the nature of man in terms of evolutionary psychology and its advocacy of the inward journey. Bly's longest and most ambitious political poem succeeds by using a strategy considerably different from that employed in his ear-lier work. When Bly placed his apocalyptic "Teeth Mother" before the more psychologically oriented poems in his 1973 book *Sleepers,* he was declaring his shift of emphasis away from the political and back to the psychospiritual.

Sleepers, Part 2:
"I Came Out of the Mother Naked"

Bly has said that his essay on the Great Mother consciousness, "I Came Out of the Mother Naked," which serves as a bridge in *Sleepers* linking "The Teeth Mother" and the poem "Sleepers," is in fact "full of mad generalizations" (*T*, 251), justified because the subject inter-ested him so much. But whatever the empirical validity of Bly's asser-tions about the origins of consciousness, his essay is extremely valuable for the reader of Bly's poetry. First of all, it explains and justifies his poetic strategy in *Sleepers,* since by positing the existence of both an individual and a national "double consciousness" (*S*, 32), the poet reconciles the seeming incompatibility between his inward, privacy poems such as "Sleepers" and his outward, political poems such as "The Teeth Mother." Second, his argument for a necessary balance between masculine and feminine consciousness within each person justifies the final poem, "Sleepers Joining Hands," as a psy-chospiritual journey toward the goal of harmonizing the two modes of consciousness in the poet himself.

Bly's essay is important also for two ancillary reasons. It identifies significant sources of theme and imagery in his poetry. The poet mentions specifically the Jungian tradition of evolutionary depth psychology, as well as the mythologies of many cultures, astrology, Tarot cards, the *I Ching,* and fairy tales from around the world. Also, the essay links mother consciousness with Bly's concept of the tripartite human brain, a structure built up through evolution into three layers—reptile, mammal, and "new" brain. Each layer has its associated values and imagery, and the necessity of communicating among the three layers encourages the contemporary, leaping poetry Bly admires as "a model of the interior of the brain." Bly believes this to be a better "model of human consciousness than the older linear poem because, as brain researchers now know, the mind evidently thinks in flashes and images" (*T*, 151–52). The style of the essay itself resembles Bly's leaping poetry. The essay moves swiftly among different worlds and categories via allusion and quotation, rather than developing a logical and linear argument such as characterized the poet's essays in the *Fifties* and the *Sixties.*

Bly begins his eight-part essay with two epigraphs. The first, from the *Tao Te Ching,* establishes two ancient, universal truths. Not only the powerful attraction of mother consciousness for men, but also the dialectical antagonism between it and masculine, or patriarchal, consciousness are as true for the Western world as for the Orient. The second epigraph, Bly's revised version of a famous passage from the Book of Job, here slyly attributed to the *"Old Testament,* restored," not only suggests that once the Mother was as powerful as the patriarchal "Lord" of the King James version, but also provides the first of the essay's many examples of Bly's willingness to make extravagant leaps of the imagination.

Part 1 discusses the historical evidence for mother culture, for the belief that social organization took the form of matriarchies in many lands before the emergence of the now-dominant patriarchies. Bly cites the work of Bachofen, a forerunner of Jung, for support, and he invokes Jung himself to argue that many of the ancient myths and legends recounting the struggle of the hero really describe "a centuries-long fight against the Mothers" (*S*, 30). In the records of this struggle, a hero was defined as any man who managed to defeat the all-powerful mother consciousness and achieve "even a slight amount of masculine consciousness." Bly cites *Beowulf* as an example. The ease with which Bly segues from the historical and external matriarchies to the timeless and inward mother consciousness, or Jungian anima, underscores his belief in the essential correspondence between culture and consciousness, between society and the individual.

Part 2 is perhaps the most important of the eight parts for the reader of the poetry, for in it Bly asserts his belief that feminine (i.e., mother) and masculine (i.e., father) consciousness coexist within each individual's psyche. Further, he catalogs a virtual iconography of images and values associated with these two complementary aspects of personality. These manifestations of mother and father consciousness occur in myth, dream, and art, including Bly's own poetry. Bly asserts that each human personality, or psyche, has two modes, "two worlds of consciousness: one world associated with the dark, and one world with the light" (*S*, 31), and this human "double consciousness" (*S*, 32) expresses itself universally in the following contrasting pairs of (Mo) Mother-(Fa) Father manifestations: (1) (Mo) the dark half of consciousness vs. (Fa) the light, white half of consciousness; (2) (Mo) first in historical development vs. (Fa) developed after a battle with the matriarchies; (3) (Mo) the Chinese *yin* vs. (Fa) the Chinese *yang*; (4) (Mo) astrology, "the great intellectual triumph of the Mother civilization" (*S*, 31); and Tarot psychology, the *I Ching,* and fairy tales—remnants of the once great mother civilization vs. (Fa) logic, empirical sciences, technology; (5) (Mo) favorite images include night, sea, animals with curving horns and cleft hooves, the moon, bundles of grain (Ceres, Demeter), the left hand; favorite creatures include turtles, owls, doves, and the oyster—"all womb-shaped, night, or ancient round sea creatures" (*S*, 32) vs. (Fa) main image is "the bright blue sky surrounding the sun—its metal then was gold" (*S*, 32); Apollo with gold rays around his head; the right hand; (6) (Mo) left brain, intuition, circles, feeling, valleys; cortex—mammal brain; affection for nature, compassion, love of water, grief and care for the dead, love of whatever is hidden, intuition, ecstasy vs. (Fa) right brain, logic, squares, thinking, mountaintops; neo-cortex—new brain; rational, ascetic, love of control, law, morality, commandments; "tries to reach the spirit through asceticism" (*S*, 32); (7) (Mo) north side of mountain (always in shadow); south side of river (always in shadow) vs. (Fa) south side of mountain (where light falls); north side of river (the light side); (8) (Mo) Indians vs. (Fa) Puritans; and (9) (Mo) acceptance of death vs. (Fa) fear of death.

Part 3 discusses the theory and imagery of man's double consciousness in terms of a specific example from American history, a formative influence upon the country's contemporary psyche. Bly presents the historical struggle of Puritans and Indians as an example of the antagonism between father consciousness and mother consciousness. The Puritan subjugation of the Indians corresponds in the individual psyche to the masculine consciousness repressing the feminine consciousness into the unconscious, merging it with the detested shadow side of the personality. Because the Puritans feared and hated their own feminine side, they found it easy and even justifiable to massacre people who lived by the laws of feminine consciousness, who even organized their society in the form of a matriarchy. This is for Bly an historical instance of the common phenomenon[9] of a person or society unconsciously projecting the psyche's conflicts onto an object in the external world. An imbalance of forces in the individual or national psyche has consequences for the external world. Here, as elsewhere, Bly is careful to assert that he is not against masculine consciousness in itself, but only against the disproportionate relationship that in today's world so often exists between it and feminine consciousness.

Part 4 begins a long discussion of the four types, the four faces, of the Great Mother. In this part Bly discusses the two mothers who exist opposite each other on the plane of physical development: the Good Mother versus the Death Mother. The next part discusses the two mothers who exist opposite each other on the plane of a person's or society's spiritual development: the Ecstatic Mother versus the Teeth Mother. Bly's justification for this discussion is that society needs to scrutinize myth, legend, dream, and art to understand these long-buried mothers, because society is presently at a turning point, moving from total domination by father consciousness to an acceptance of mother consciousness. When a culture or individual starts to return to the mother, says Bly, they must descend blindly through layers of buried consciousness into the collective unconscious. They may encounter any one of the four mothers first, since they "cannot have one of the mothers without having them all" (*S*, 34). Since two of the mothers are benevolent and two are dangerous, it is important to be aware of all the possibilities. The Good Mother–Death Mother pair, and their domain of the natural world, is less important in *Sleepers* than it is in the books of prose poems which follow it.

Part 5 discusses the two aspects of the Great Mother most important to the essentially spiritual world of *Sleepers:* the Ecstatic Mother and the Teeth mother. The Ecstatic Mother is a muse, often pictured dancing, and in her teens or early twenties. She is associated with the goddesses Artemis, Diotima, and Sophia, and with the virgin mothers, because "her main job was not to bring children into the world, but to bring ecstasy into the world" (S, 39). All poems come from the energy of the Ecstatic Mother, for "all creativity lies in the feminine consciousness" (S, 40). Bly cites Leonardo and Dante as men who were drawn toward poetry and ecstasy through contact with the Ecstatic Mother, whether in their imagination or in the form of a living Beatrice.

The Teeth Mother, also known as the Stone Mother, is the most fearsome of the four mothers. She has the power to stop "the developing male consciousness in its tracks" (S, 41), to turn it to stone, like a Medusa head. Her teeth signify the dismembering of the human psyche, and Bly suggests that her special fierceness comes perhaps from her association with a specific time in history. This speculation underscores Bly's belief that the origins and development of individual and collective consciousness can be linked to specific periods of human evolutionary history, as in his comment that "the Stone Mother perhaps represents in history the Mother culture during the time it was implacably hostile to the masculine consciousness" (S, 42). And the return of this Mother at a later historical period is also emphasized by Bly, for "American fate is to face this Mother before other Industrial nations" (S, 41). Bly concludes with a litany of examples of the Teeth and Death Mothers in contemporary American culture.

The conclusion of the essay emphasizes Bly's commitment to Jung's psychospiritual goals of personality development. Bly avers that his "psychic archaeology" (S, 49) to rediscover and return to mother consciousness is an attempt to overcome the prevalent contemporary despising of "the anima, the feminine soul" (S, 49). He acknowledges personal reasons for wanting to do this, casting himself as a typical product of "the patriarchal and Protestant heritage of northern Europe" (S, 49) that settled America. He underscores again the essay's pervasive debt to a Jungian tradition that includes Bachofen, Neumann, and Esther Harding. But the place of honor in this conclusion to the essay is reserved for Jung himself, whose long quotation draws on the poetic images of the ruined house of rationalism and the nourishing water of the unconscious, images central to Bly's own poetry, to urge mankind to undertake a psychospiritual quest for a balanced psyche, one granting equal status to masculine and feminine consciousness. Bly ends this essay, and prepares for the long autobiographical poem to follow, by endorsing the spirtual quest which Jung's quote advocates. Bly sees this inward quest as central to "my own poems and the poems of so many other poets alive now" (*S*, 50), which seek to rediscover "parts in us that are linked with music, with solitude, water, trees, the parts that grow when we are far from the centers of ambition."

Sleepers Joining Hands, Part 3:
"Sleepers Joining Hands: A Long Poem"

The title poem of the book, "Sleepers Joining Hands," marks a significant change in Bly's career. It is not only a turning away from political poetry, but also a turning toward a poetry that will be simultaneously more private and more personal than the lyrics of *Silence in the Snowy Fields*. In this poem Bly attempts to ground his personal experience in a collective one; and in order to accomplish this he describes his personal development in full-blown overtly mythic allusions and archetypcal symbols, very different from *Silence's* minimalist imagery, whose phenomenological resonance was suggestive of a deeper, but largely unspecified universal meaning. Bly described "Sleepers Joining Hands" as an "autobiographical poem" (*T*, 257) written over a four-year period. This version contains only 480 of the 5,000 lines he wrote for it, because "4500 were written by some other part of me, or my memory—they didn't have the [psychic] tone!" (*T*, 136). In 1981 an interviewer revealed that Bly "is still revising it and trying to come to terms with a much longer version (about ten thousand lines) that he wrote during the early seventies."[10] The length, the autobiographical nature, the evolving composition, and especially the sustained use of the Jungian paradigm of human personality to structure the poem—all these features set "Sleepers" apart from Bly's earlier work. The poem presents a poet-hero's journey on a psychic quest in search of selfhood[11] and full membership in a community imaged as "sleepers joining hands," the human race, past and present, united by the hero's own achievement of a harmony within himself between the conscious and the unconscious aspects of his personality, his psyche.

Though "Sleepers" is a long poem built from parts written over a long period of time and published separately in various places, the poem seems unified. Perhaps the major reason is that it keeps as a constant referent the language and ideas of a developed, mature philosophy of human personality. Bly's willingness to invoke another's philosophy in his poetry is a sign of strength, of the poet's increasing sureness that his own voice, distinctive and mature in this poem, will not be drowned out by another's words. It is as though the facility Bly gained in handling the dangerous, potentially enervating language of politics in his Vietnam poetry had emboldened him to wrestle the angel of philosophical poetry—a far more dangerous foe because for Bly it seems appealingly seductive rather than antagonistic. Yet he manages to strengthen and deepen his music in this and later poetry by his belief in and judicious use of the language and ideas of Carl Jung.

Jungian Psychology and "Sleepers"

Bly's poem cannot be fully understood, let alone appreciated, without some knowledge of the concepts of Jungian psychology the poet invokes in his poem. Naturally, there will be reader resistance to any poem so heavily indebted to a system of reference that is not a universally recognized part of the culture. But one result of the fragmentation of twentieth-century culture is precisely this persistent search by arists for systems of reference that have any currency at all, such as Eliot's classical allusions, Yeats's gyres, and Joyce's *Ulysses*.[12] "Sleepers," too, encompasses far more than its Jungianism; but it is both misleading and wrong to claim that it does not "accord with a Jungian schema."[13] The proof of this is that the most illuminating articles[14] on the poem all derive their strength from using Jung to understand what Bly is doing. In particular, there are three basic concepts with which the reader should be familiar if he is to understand the poem. They involve the structure, the development, and the goals of human personality.

According to Jung, an individual's personality is the totality of the individual's consciousness (experiences he is aware of), his personal unconscious (experiences he has suppressed or forgotten), and the collective unconscious (inherited universal characteristics and wisdom, gleaned from the evolutionary experiences of mankind and passed down to each individual). The picture Bly presents of his hero in this personal epic is drawn from all three of these sources; and the progress of the poem is based on the dramatic interaction of all three of these aspects of the hero's personality. The goal of personality development, indeed of life itself, is to integrate and harmonize all three aspects in one personality.

Perhaps more than any other twentieth-century psychologist, Jung believed that the development of an individual's personality depended as much on strong innate forces as it did on external influences—on nature as much as nurture. In the unconscious there are powerful complexes of forces, called archetypes, which, when activated within an individual's personality, often cluster around and find formal expression through an archetypal symbol. An archetype is not a symbol, but an inherited, originally unconscious psychic pattern that, when activated, can exert force upon, and even take dominion over, a person's psyche. An archetype sometimes generates an archetypal symbol in order to manifest itself to the conscious mind, which would otherwise be unware of it. The emergence of an archetypal symbol from the collective unconscious into the conscious, usually through dreams, always heralds a moment of potential personality transformation and growth. The persona, the anima, the shadow, the wise old man, and the self are important complexes and archetypes in Bly's poem.

The persona is the totality of all the masks the conscious mind assumes to deal with the world's collective consciousness, the various faces one learns to present to the public. As Jung at one point explained, "the persona is a complicated system of relations between the individual consciousness and society, fittingly enough a kind of mask," designed for two purposes. On the one hand it serves "to make a definite impression upon others, and, on the other, to conceal the true nature of the individual."[15] In Bly's poem, as in society in general, the persona is overdeveloped in relation to the other forces in the psyche in the typical twentieth-century individual. Thus it has become a threat to the anima, the archetype symbolizing the feminine soul, the individual "in his relationship to the collective unconscious."[16] In Jung's schema the persona and the anima have "a compensatory relationship"[17] that needs to be kept in balance. The opening predicament of "Sleepers" finds the feminine anima "chained" in a personality dominated by the overdeveloped persona.

The shadow archetype is, in a sense, the opposite of the persona. It is the dark side of man, the one he hides and, all too often, denies and represses because it contains all the materials that are incompatible with his chosen conscious attitude. As Jung describes it, "the shadow personifies everything that the subject refuses to acknowledge about himself."[18] It includes man's instinctuality, his animal nature, but also the beneficial powers of intuition and creativity. When the ego and the shadow are creatively aligned, then the individual can use the considerable energies of the shadow to expand his consciousness, to be more vital, to grow. It is this alignment of consciousness with unconscious energies that redoubles them and generates, in Bly's phrase, "the light around the body." As Jung noted, when the shadow is repressed into the unconscious, rather than "made conscious so as to produce a tension of opposites, without which no forward movement is possible," then consciousness itself "is doomed to stagnation, congestion, and ossification. Life is born only of the spark of opposites."[19] In Bly's poem the shadow's energies are projected upon, and thus imagistically associated with Indians, blacks, and nature in general, with whom the exclusively rational persona so often denies any affinity or even relationship. Society's one-sided education of the hero's persona, and the consequent repression of his shadow, are the actions lamented in "The Shadow Goes Away," part 1 of Bly's poem.

The wise old man who appears in part 2, "Meeting the Man Who Warns Me," represents in Jung the archetypal guide sent from the unconscious to lead the conscious hero to a greater understanding of himself. In the poem the hero meets and acknowledges the power of the archetypal wise man, and this acknowledgment allows the wise man's voice to speak through the hero, to describe an archetypal experience known to the hero through his collective unconscious but not through any personal experience he has had. This archetypal experience is the three-day journey of death and resurrection described in part 3, "The Night Journey in the Cooking Pot."

This example of the poet remembering something before he actually experiences it in the poem illustrates an important aspect of the archetypes and the collective unconscious in forming human personality. They not only can illuminate something that has happened in the past to the individual or the species, but they also can prefigure and predict events that will happen to an individual in the future. For Jung, human knowledge does not come solely, or even mainly, from external forces (experience) impinging on and altering our consciousness. Rather, man has innate knowledge, stored in the collective unconscious, that sometimes emerges and predisposes him to be especially receptive toward, or even to seek out, a certain experience. This inward world is a timeless world, and thus different from the usually linear time of a narrative. For Jung a man's psychic life is governed not only by events that happened to his ancestors, or to himself

as a child, or yesterday, but also by events toward which his development is moving, events in the future. Thus in this poem, Bly's hero
knows the night journey before he actually experiences it.

Finally, the archetype of self is especially important to Bly's poem.
The self is the archetype of wholeness, of complementary harmony between the conscious and unconscious elements of the psyche. Jung described it as embracing "not only the conscious but also the
unconscious psyche, and is therefore, so to speak, a personality which
we *also* are."[20] The self represents the goal of personality development, life's goal. However, the complete achievement of selfhood is
quite rare, approximated most closely, according to Jung, by enlight-
ened religious figures such as Christ or Buddha. The very existence of
these figures symbolizes also man's universal belief in the goal of selfhood. Bly's poem is an epic describing the quest to achieve selfhood,
and everything that happens to the poem's hero must be finally understood in terms of its relationship to this struggle.

For both Jung and Bly the task of human personality is its evolving
development toward selfhood. The process of individuation, by which
the person gains increasing awareness and experience of his complex
psyche and moves toward ever greater integration and harmonization
of conscious and unconscious material, is the process of growing toward selfhood The individuation process tends toward a psychoreligious goal, the discovery of twofold consciousness within the
individual and the revelation of a brotherhood not only among all humans but also with all other conscious things, even including rocks
and other forms of so-called inanimate matter. This discovery evokes
the recognition of the God within his creation, or what Bly, following an ancient tradition, called the soul of the world. In this poem
the religious images (Christ, the King, Herod, the manger, and circumcision), though drawn from orthodox religions, are all used to express this archetypal, psychoreligious sense. Indeed, the poem's title
suggests the religious sense of unity among all men, coming from
their shared unconscious, the dreams that each enters every night to
discover anew his brotherhood, to join hands with all other "Sleepers," both the living and the dead.

The Poetics of Bly's "Long Poem"

The poetics of "Sleepers" is very different from the private voice
and deep image of the lyrics of *Silence,* or the public voice and the

psychohistorical image of the dark satires of *Light*. Bly's poetics in "Sleepers" is influenced by his wish to fulfill a particularly prevalent twentieth-century desire: to write a long poem. Bly uses several strategies for extending the poem beyond the limits of the personal lyric— for expanding the range of subject matter and universalizing the experience recounted in his autobiographical long poem. Three of his most important strategies to do this are his use of an epic framework as a structuring principle, his use of a dramatic element in the narrative progression, and his use of a private symbolism, generated mainly from Jungian concepts and terminology, whose full significance can gradually emerge for the reader within the expansive context of a long poem.

The "long poem" form is a twentieth-century hybrid of two genres, the narrative epic and the personal lyric. The essential feature of this hybrid is that the poet present his personal experience, his autobiography, as a synecdoche of life in his time. Thus if he is not a "hero" in the traditional sense of a man larger-than-life, a magnified representation of the achievements and aspirations of a particular culture and people, at least this twentieth-century hero can be recognized as one of a type familiar enough to be acknowledged as in some sense universal. Similarly, the poet and his poem must look outward, offering his life as a significant experience to all other people in the community. Unlike the traditional epic, in which the hero's awareness of himself as a representative of the culture is largely overshadowed by his deeds, the modern personal epic is marked precisely by the hero's self-conscious effort to present himself as representative of something larger than the individual, larger than any deed he might possibly perform except the one heroic act left open to modern man, to rediscover himself. Thus, from Whitman on it is the act of self-creation through self-discovery, usually embodied in a poem, that is the central heroic act of the modern epic. The modern hero seeks to discover in his own particular life the universal factor that will allow him to escape the solipsistic, alienated condition of the isolate man and to see the world as a community (the subject of the traditional epic). In Bly's poem the community of man is based on the common inheritance of the collective unconscious, which unites all people whether they recognize it or not. This is the basis for Bly's ultimate affirmation in the poem's last line, "All the sleepers in the world join hands." In this regard Bly's epic is philosophically grounded in twentieth-century depth psychology, especially Jung's concept of the collective unconscious, much as Dante's epic is grounded in thirteenth-century Christianity.

Though dealing with a modern subject, Bly is not afraid to use traditional epic conventions to structure his poem; indeed, he might well argue that the traditional epic is an invention that symbolizes an archetypal urge in the collective unconscious, and its conventions are therefore not arbitrary but right and proper in a deep psychological sense. Therefore, for a modern poet to use them again is no more than appropriate, especially in an epic whose subject is the elucidation of the universal aspect of personality. Bly uses such epic conventions as the hero's descent into the underworld (here called the Night Journey in the Cooking Pot), the intervention of the gods (here called archetypal figures, such as the shadow and the wise old man), the paralleling of this epic with others in a discernible tradition (Joseph Campbell is helpful in explaining Bly's biblical allusions to Joseph in the Well, to Jonah's death and resurrection in the whale, and to Christ's life),[21] and the climactic goal of the discovery/redemption of the entire world by the hero's achievement. Bly's hero successfully performs the unifying act that characterizes the modern long poem/epic: he discovers a unitive relationship between consciousness and unconsciousness in man's personality, between man and nature, and between life and death.

"Sleepers Joining Hands: A Long Poem": A Reading

"The Shadow Goes Away," the first part of Bly's epic "Long Poem," begins in the middle of things, with six lines delineating the present psychic state of the narrator. His masculine, persona-dominated "I" is separated from his feminine, mother consciousness, symbolized as "The woman chained to the shore," an allusion to the Andromeda myth so aptly explained by Bly's mentor, Joseph Campbell.[22] He recognizes, and fears, the psychic death such fragmentation threatens ("the light gone out of the body"), and thus both masculine "I" and the enchained feminine consciousness (Jung's "persona" and "anima," here combined as "us") await the incoming tide and emergence of an archetypal force from out of the threatening but potentially liberating oceanic unconscious. The scene dramatizes the beginning of a psychic journey toward the integration of the narrator's now-separate parts, referred to here as "I," "the woman," and the suppressed shadow that the title indicates has gone away. An ominous note, signaling the peril of such a psychic trip, reverberates from the juxtaposition of the fledgling narrator ("without feathers") and a "blood-colored moon gobbling up the sand," a note recalling the Teeth Mother's apocalyptic visage. The antagonism at this stage of the journey between masculine "I" and mother consciousness within the narrator finds a corresponding image in nature, an owl landing with "claws out" to repel the alien, masculine presence in its nest; throughout Bly's poem such conjoining of wings with claws calls up the destructive, nonnurturing face of the Mother.

The remaining sixty-nine lines of this first part of Bly's long poem presents the narrator's dream-memory of how he came to such a conflicting, dangerous state; they are meant to typify the psychic inheritance and education of a contemporary American. Bly not only limns the formative influences on the development of his contemporary hero, especially the social and political environment from which he must individuate himself, but also presents a larger picture of the fragmented contemporary psyche that the hero must integrate. To draw this picture, the poet introduces a number of the poem's major sources and motifs: biblical archetypal symbolism ("I show the father the coat stained with goat's blood"), historical allusion ("the Sioux," "Stanley's visit to Africa," "humpbacked Puritan ministers," "the Marines," and the lunar "Sea of Tranquility"), a personal history ("Men bound my shadow. That was in high school," and "on 66th Street I noticed he was gone"), and Jungian psychology ("The shadow goes away, / we are left alone in the father's house," and "the great cooking iron in which my shadow was boiling," and "the suppressed race returns: snakes and transistors filling the beaches").

This last image, concluding part 1, returns us to the moon-lit beaches of the first six lines, and to the narrator's psychic quest in the present. The return of the repressed, foreshadowed by the "blood-colored moon" in line 6, has achieved full bloom, with the repressed mother consciousness returning wearing the destructive masks of the Teeth Mother and Death Mother. The threatened destruction of the last lines of part 1 is imaged in social and political terms. It is certainly significant that this is the last time in Bly's longest poem that his imagination calls on imagery from the public and political worlds—which had provided so much of the imagery, language, and voice of his previous book, *The Light around the Body*. Part 1 of this epic poem marks not only the narrator's individuation, but also the poet's, beyond the sociopolitical concerns that inspired him during the Vietnam War period. The terms of his poetry, and of his hero's psychic exploration, will from this moment on be more personal than political. In these concluding images of part 1, the attack of the returning, repressed feminine aspect of psyche is a necessary prelude to its integration with the heretofore repressive masculine consciousness, what Bly termed the yin-yang of the human psyche. A death leading to resurrection, a purgation of the psyche's present fragmentation and antagonisms ("divorced men and women drown"), are a necessary preparation for the psychic marriage and unity necessary to whatever selfhood is to follow. All the enmity that the masculine showed against the feminine in the slaughter of the Sioux, the "Shadowy People" who protected and educated the narrator's abandoned shadow "brother," is answered in full by the return of the "suppressed race" in the guise of the destructive Mothers. But the narrator-hero, after his experience of the education recounted in his symbolic dream-memory, is empowered to refuse the money of the Marines, to recognize it as symbolic of the psychic suicide of an overdominant masculine consciousness. His knowledge enables him to do something America itself could not: "turn and leave" the Vietnam debacle. He is "flying" now, not the fledgling of the first six lines, and he is ready to journey further into his own psyche.

Part 2, "Meeting the Man Who Warns Me," begins like the first, with the narrator describing his psychic state in terms of his relationship with a woman symbolic of his own feminine consciousness. She "urges me to speak truths," and his conversation with his feminine side signals a new state of mutual awareness, rather than the antagonism that began part 1. Similarly, the talking of the owls and loons in this beginning stanza reflects the narrator's new state of sensitivity to such "fragments of the mother," though he acknowledges that his new state is only half aware, as "half or more of the moon rolls on in shadow."

But this part of the poem is not to be a catalog of images of mother consciousness, but rather a series of steps descending into deeper levels of the narrator's psyche. There he encounters the "man who warns me" to "talk to me about your life, or turn back" from the psychic quest. This part opens with the narrator waking to a perception of his life in archetypal images, rather than the previously employed sociopolitical terms: "I wake and find myself in the woods, far from the castle." This initial metaphor of the hero's psychic state, drawing

upon the worlds of dream, fairy tale, and myth for its terms, is
echoed at the end of this part of the poem, when the hero feels "like
a King coming to his own shores." The narrator even seems to begin
to differentiate his speaking "I," his ego, from his unconscious, "the
sleeper," who "turns to the wall" in line 3 and begins to dream.

Here in part 2 the shifts from waking to dreaming become more
problematical, as a simplistic division of human consciousness into either dreaming or waking gives way to a recognition of consciousness
as a many-layered phenomenon (as in "the body surrounds me" or the
narrator's dream within a dream after meeting the "man from a
milder planet"). Bly needs this multilevel model to express the various stages of his psychic growth. Rather than symbolize them in different myth-stories, Bly implicitly invokes his theory of the
multilayered "three brains" (cf. *Leaping Poetry*), whose activity is a
continual leaping from state to state and back again. When Bly writes
"I dream" or "I wake" in this poem, it is as though he is invoking
another verbal mood, one termed the "three brain conditional,"
which he uses to express a truth of psychic life that exists both always
and sometimes, apart from the past-present-future time frame inherent in logical, causal relationships. In other words, the dreams do not
serve mainly to illuminate or qualify a waking reality—the dream life
is as real as waking life, and "I dream" is just a convention to signal
the narrator's passage to a new stage of meditation, a shift of psychic
state.

Before the narrator can meet "the man who warns me" he must
descend beneath the overdominant rational father consciousness that
creates an imbalance in the psyche of contemporary man ("I dream
that the fathers are dying"). He follows the energy that rises from
under the earth, from under his masculine consciousness, by descending to the sources of collective racial memory ("down the damp steps
of the Tigris") and personal memory ("the darkness we saw outside
the cradle"):

> Something white calls to us:
> it is the darkness we saw outside the cradle.
> My shadow is underneath me,
> floating in the dark, in his small boat bobbing among reeds.
> A fireball floats in the corner of the Eskimo's house—
> It is a light that comes nearer when called!
> A light the spirits turn their heads for,

suddenly shining over land and sea!
I taste the heaviness of the dream,
the northern lights curve up toward the roof of my mouth.
The energy is inside us. . . .
I start toward it, and I meet an old man.

The narrator recognizes this dark shadow as part of himself ("underneath me"), even fundamental and supportive of his conscious life. The darkness of this unknown which he penetrates in his descent becomes "white," a "light that comes nearer when called!" The shared activity of "floating" unites this shadow of the narrator with the "fireball" of the next line, so that the darkness of the unconscious becomes paradoxically inseparable from this radiant light the spirits "turn their heads for, / suddenly shining over land and sea!" Most importantly, the narrator discovers that this light/energy is not outside himself, but within. The discovery is crucial in Bly's epic poem, and the metaphor to express it reflects its importance: the narrator is the world itself, and the energy is imaged as the cosmic energy of "the northern lights." That the energy arches through the mouth is a subtle reminder that this poem is, finally, about the development of a speaking poet. The narrator's discovery of the inwardness of the light impels him to further exploration; but his way is blocked by the archetypal "old man," who makes a demand that threatens to halt the narrator's entire psychic quest for selfhood. The old man figure, described by Campbell as a symbol of the supportive yet disturbingly unsettling power and wisdom in the narrator's own unconscious,[23] forces him to a painful yet joyous reexamination and reconfiguration of his own psychic history: "I am here. Either talk to me about your life, or turn back."

The passage in which the hero emboldens himself to push on in his psychic quest, to accept the old man's challenge, is equally strong, and in image and tone looks forward to the psalmlike voice of part 4. He recounts the power of things known only by inference ("So much just beyond the reach of our eyes") and the enduring presence of the archetypal unconscious ("what cannot be remembered and cannot be forgotten"), poignantly imagining the sense of loss that hovers over both his collective and personal unconscious as "the chaff blowing about my father's feet." He sees in nature evidence of consciousness, of creatures obeying an innate purpose: "the night frogs who give out the croak of the planet turning, / the great knees of the horses loyal

to the earth risen in their will." This recognition awakens him to his
own twofold consciousness, especially its dark side, which links man
to nature's purposeful passion. The narrator speaks in the voice of the
"dark spirit" he had previously denied, and he describes his life in
archetypal images of psychic death and rebirth. He likens himself to
Jonah, the Old Testament prophet who tried to hide from God to
avoid prophesying, but instead died and was reborn in three days
from the belly of a whale. He recounts his psychic journey to date,
how he symbolically descended "under the earth through the night-
water," and then returned transformed, reborn as "a boy who had
never seen the sea!" He compares himself in this reborn stage to "a
King coming to his own shores," an image with subtle allusions to
other archetypal epic heroes, Odysseus and Jesus Christ. The last
three lines hint at circumcision as the rite of passage, a wound that
brings joy. This passage, this rebirth, "is like wounds at sea," like
the necessary punishment/death that preceded Jonah's and the narrator's resurrection.

Part 3, "The Night Journey in the Cooking Pot," consists of six
sections, separated by asterisks. In its entirety, this part explores the
narrator's psychic state, during the periods when he has united his
conscious and unconscious parts. The "night journey" of the title is,
as Joseph Campbell describes it, a well-known metaphor for an important stage in the exploration of the unconscious.[24] The journey's
end, and the discovery of the essential unity of conscious and unconscious is beautifully expressed: "For we are like the branch bent in
the water . . . / Taken out, it is whole, it was always whole. . . ."
The sureness of tone and the successful interweaving of the personal
and the psychological in this part recall the "Six Winter Privacy
Poems" that began this book. Indeed, privacy is declared to be a
"need," and a "winter of privacy" is the image in section 3 for the
gestation period necessary for rebirth into unified consciousness. The
sleep of gestation is variously alluded to in part 3: by "the men who
drift, asleep, for three nights" (section 1), "a smile falls over the face,
the eyes fall" (4), "Deep in the mountain the sleeper is glad" (4), and
"Holy ones with eyes closed" (4). The gestation period is associated
with the kind of "sleep" referred to in the poem's (and book's) title,
and the fruitfulness that follows it is the ecstasy of leaping, dancing,
singing, and writing poetry. The sharing in the collective racial
memory, especially sharing in the wisdom of another's consciousness,

is what characterizes this sleep, and what serves to unite all persons who have experienced it, as Bly's concluding line to the whole poem suggests: "All the sleepers in the world join hands."

Section 1 declares the need for privacy and being "alone" on this journey in the "cooking pot," an image suggesting not only a rendering, purifying process but also a return to and a rebirth out of the womb of mother consciousness. The mammal whale, an animal associated in Bly's writing with the mother, protects the narrator, carries him safely through "the mouse-killing waters," as earlier in part 1 he had been able to fly over the "rat" nests in the Josephine forests.

Section 2 describes a Breughelesque winter scene symbolic of the narrator's newfound ecstasy. Birds "leap" and sing in a tree high above mice who "run dragging their tails"; the narrator too is in the tree, where "Sitting I leap from branch to branch." He is free of both gravity and the constraints of a rationalistic world view that in Bly's schema (cf. "The Three Brains") corresponds to absolute space, absolute time, and absolute simultaneity, which he defies here by simultaneously sitting and leaping. His new state is characterized also by a new role for the archetypal "old man" who threatened and "warned" him in part 2. Here that figure celebrates the hero's transformation and liberation from a dominant masculine consciousness, imaged as "deer antlers abandoned in the snow"; the archetypal wise old man calls out "long prayers at dawn," thanksgiving at the successful conclusion of the epic "night journey."

Section 3 describes the narrator's peace of mind achieved by his transformation; he floats "in solitude," having discovered "the inward path" once again, and with it an accompanying "certainty," akin to that of animals following their natural rhythms. This certainty is expressed at the end of the section in images that echo similar passages in parts 2, 4, and 5 that also serve to describe the psychic development in which consciousness of nature verges on participation in a spiritual/divine consciousness of the whole world. This section also invokes the narrator's own personal history, the discovery of "the inward path" in Bly's lonely years in New York; his mentor in this first experience of inwardness was another poet, Rilke (perhaps in the "great room" of the New York Public Library). Bly's writings in *Leaping Poetry* and *News* make clear the role of Rilke in the poetic tradition of twofold consciousness. Indeed, the penultimate image of this long poem, the panther of consciousness, comes from one of

Rilke's poems which Bly has translated. Here the images of "the wings brushing the floors of the dark" and "the face shining far inside the mountain" recall other poems of Rilke.

Section 4 describes the narrator's psychic movement from peace to joy, from discovery of the essential if elusive unity of consciousness and unconsciousness to the celebration of it in dancing, song, and poetry. The joy arrives like a call from the intelligence of nature, "a radio signal from inside a tree trunk"; and the narrator smiles and shuts his eyes, shutting down his conscious persona so that he can listen to a new voice speaking within him. "Someone is asleep in the back of my house" suggests the narrator is two persons at once, like the man who was both sitting and leaping in section 2. A long, dreamlike, surrealistic passage follows, describing the leaping from one level of the brain to another that accompanies, signals, the descent into more fundamental levels of being, a descent that takes the hero "Deep in the mountain." The hero's descent corresponds to processes in nature itself, as "The tree" becomes "naked" and joyful only after "Leaves fall in the tomby wood." This stripping process climaxes with the speaker declaring his freedom from things, for "suddenly" the Ecstatic Mother, the Muse and her dancers, appear; and the speaker starts to sing, desires to reverse the descent and "rise far into the piney top." He now realizes that, paradoxically, descent preceded resurrection ("I am not going farther from you, / I am coming nearer"); and he sees that as a poet, in his work, he loves the unconscious (and perhaps even the reader): "I never knew that I loved you until I was swallowed by the invisible." The "you" here is both the unconscious life and, through the collective memory in which all the sleepers in the world join hands, the reader as well. The unity he has discovered is not only within himself but also between himself and other people, even between himself and nature.

Section 5 of "Night Journey in the Cooking Pot" opens with the separation of the narrrator's "I" and his body, a new stage of his psychic life that signals a falling away from the ecstatic union achieved in section 4. The body is at odds with the speaking "I," and an impediment to the narrator's following of the road of inward psychic development. In words that resonate with Bly's voluminous attack on the Cartesian mind-body dualism (cf. *News of the Universe*), the hero faces an impasse to further growth: "I think I am the body, / the body rushes in and ties me up." The strong wings that carried him above the Josephine forests in part 1 of the poem, earlier in this part imaged as marvellous "great wings sweeping along the floor," have now become "clumsy wings," as the psychic flight has faltered. Nevertheless, this passage confirms the narrator's knowledge of the ecstatic union of twofold consciousness possible, even as it describes its loss; "I know what I must do, / I am ashamed looking at the fish in the water" invokes all the glory earlier associated with the night journey of Jonah, the night-water of the Tigris, and the serenity of the "vast halls inside the heads of animals." The final stanza of this section uses a biblical allusion to express the timeless mind-body antagonism that the psychic quest for rebirth must always overcome. The "King," like Herod, senses the newborn child's first breath in "the manger hay," even though he is "a hundred miles away," and he sends his minions to murder the Infant King, for "there cannot be two rulers in one body." Rationalism's instinct is "to kill the child in the old moonlit villages of the brain." The final section of part 4 expresses the narrator's return to wakefulness ("sitting on the edge of my bed") and its attendant dominant masculine consciousness. The "mind waters" of his newly won unity of consciousness spill out "on the rug." The narrator is no longer "free"; instead, he is like "those who run large railroads at dusk," doing the work of the father culture. He leaves behind the Ecstatic Mother when "I decide that death is friendly"; the transformation of the narrator back to a rationalistic, masculine and persona-dominant consciousness ("I fall into my own hands") is accompanied by images of death and continuing antagonism within the narrator between mother and father consciousness ("whole towns of singing women carrying to the burial fields the look I saw on my father's face," the look of unrelenting opposition to evidence of mother consciousness in his "son"). The third part of Bly's long poem concludes with the narrator unhappy with his present state of being ("I hit my own body"), angry at his "betrayal" of the unity of consciousness he had discovered/achieved earlier, and dissatisfied with his poetry for its failure to "help" either himself or the community. He is both "ashamed" and wide awake, and the night journey of death and resurrection seems to him now very far away.

Part 4, "Water Drawn Up Into the Head," images in its title the union of the unconscious ("water") with the mind ("the head"), and it is a reflection upon the lesson learned in the first three parts of the poem, especially in the preceding "Night Journey." The hero, now speaking from a position of experience and wisdom, reflects on his achievement of unity of consciousness and declares that he can have a similar experience again. The tone is one of measured confidence and optimism; the narrator addresses the readers ("you") and links himself with them ("we," "our") in a way that marks the end of the intensely personal account of the psychic quest in the first three parts of the poem. Further, the religious imagery imbues the quest with a psychospiritual dimension. The tone of reflection is established in the beginning, in the italicized parable about a man who made a journey to claim his inheritance, and then returned home. The parallel with the hero's psychic journey to reclaim his lost mother consciousness and bring it "home," integrate it into his conscious self, is obvious. The traveler has learned about both the goals and the journey to it. The goal is unity of self, coming "face to face" with "you," the spiritually imbued energy within each person; this encounter makes "glad" the "holder" (not a "be-holder," since the object seen is also the object seeing, one part of the self recognizing another part as itself). The hero's cosmic "laugh" of acceptance, like that of the "mad condor" and also "the men who laugh all night in their sleep," acknowledges this recognition. The narrator declares himself in this state both "passive" and "divine," a pure "consciousness" sweeping out over the fields like "a revolving beacon" in the night. This reconciliation of masculine and feminine consciousness is imaged in terms that recall another aspect of the biblical story of King Herod and Jesus used at the end of part 3, for here the Passover is invoked in the reference to "the wing of affection passes over." The enmity of the masculine and feminine is reconciled in the image of "flying bulls glimpsed passing the moon disc," an improvement over the moon half "in shadow" that signalled the psychic state of part two.

Here the hero's remembrance of his achievement of unified consciousness empowers him to speak a long paean to the God-like force in the universe, the "curved energy" that is discoverable within each person. He begins by scrutinizing other definitions of God. First, he considers the material world, "with all its visible stars." It is a "great tomb," perhaps a monument to the existence of God, but it "is not God." Second, he thinks of ghosts and other minor, localized spirits, "but everyone knows they are not God." He firmly denies that Christ, "who raised the dead and started time," should be identified with God. Fourth, he considers the social/moral good of community and brotherly love, often posited as an ethical absolute in lieu of any God, and he praises it for helping mankind "faintly" when the other forms of spiritual energy are dead ("When the waterholes go"). But better than arguing about these definitions of God, says the narrator, is to discover the true "river" in which to lose oneself, the Ur-river Tigris flowing with the "curved energy." The hero himself felt this force ("I entered that energy one day"), and he associates it with the energy of the collective unconscious, imaged as the ancient Tigris that nourished the very cradle of civilization, in the final line of "Sleepers." As with the sacrament of baptism, which this immersion in the river suggests, to lose one's self is a necessary stage in the struggle to find one's self, the "you" within each person. This "you" for whom "We have no name," a God hidden from sight, is known only indirectly, by inference of an invisible cause from invisible effects; and the hero describes him in psalmlike language as he who "makes grass grow upon mountains," who feeds the "dark cattle of the sea," who "feeds the young ravens who call on him," a patriarchal spirit ("he") supportive of the creatures dear to and symbolic of the anima (including the young raven symbolic of the poet himself). This gentle affirmation recalls Bly's declaration at the end of the Great Mother essay that the ideal personality is one "balanced" between masculine and feminine, a counterpoised yin-yang.

The concluding section of part 4 begins with the pluperfect tense, "I have sat here alone," and collapses time (two hours—two years) to suggest the ever-presence of "another being living inside me." The knowledge gained from the psychic trip makes the narrator confident that though the "other being" may not be as intensely felt as in the ecstatic moments of part 3, still he is ever-present, both within ("He is looking out of my eyes") and without ("I hear him / in the wind through the bare trees"). This other being is then imaged archetypally, as "the King" who once promised the hero purification through pain ("more pain than wounds at sea"). The "other being" is a simultaneous projection and expression of the narrator himself, in his achieved selfhood, all parts at once integrated; there is also the suggestion of a divine "other being," a force larger than but not limited to the speaker himself, a force whose effects are evident in both man and the material world. In its modern tentativeness at thinking of divinity, Bly's invocation of this "other being" is strangely reminiscent of Eliot's reference to a similarly imagined "other being" ("who is this third who walks beside us") in *The Waste Land*. Images of death and descent ("fall," "the thick leaves fall, / falling past their own trunk") are, paradoxically, welcomed, for they herald the resurrection to come. The hero himself becomes explicitly identified with the tree in the poem's conclusion, dropping his leaves and becoming "naked," effacing his persona and "leaving only the other one." But this one is heard "in the wind through the bare trees," which is to say in the spirit moving among those who have stripped themselves of their ego flowers. Thus Bly's contemporary poet-hero, the man who has struggled for selfhood, has become a new incarnation of the ancient Aeolian harp, that wonderful instrument capable of transforming the universe's curved energy into music.

Section 4, "An Extra Joyful Chorus for Those Who Have Read This Far," is an appendix to the psychic quest of the first four parts of "Sleepers Joining Hands," a "joyful chorus" in two senses of the word: it echoes the images and themes of the poem proper, and it expands in singing fashion on the cosmic, paradoxical nature of consciousness. The first stanza names "the mysterious mother" as the source of the "call" to psychic struggle and quest. The narrator, now at odds with himself ("not floating, but fighting"), answers the call by leaping again with his masculine consciousness ("my sword") into the mother's ocean-nest ("mouth full of seaweed"). The lines recall the image of the owl approaching his nest "claws out" at the beginning of "The Shadow Goes Away"; and they recall also Bly's comment on the hero-dragon fight in *Beowulf* in "I Came Out of the Mother Naked": "The dragon in inner life is man's fear of women, and in public life it is the matriarchy's conservative energy" (*S*, 30). The archetypal battle between masculine and feminine consciousness begins anew. The next stanza presents a catalog of images which use hints of myth, religion, fairy tales, and nature worship—all cited by Jung and Bly as reservoirs of collective memory—to describe the narrator's attraction toward the mother and toward his own rebirth in "new water." These images are powerful, especially when read in the context of their use throughout Bly's work. The narrator seems to acknowledge this in the next quatrain, referring to discoveries made over again by the poet reading "my own poems late at night." This positive attitude contrasts with the poet-narrator's despair at the end of part 3, "what I have written is not good enough." Here he rediscovers in his poetry both the "road" of inwardness and "the naked thing above" invoked at the end of part 4—Bly's two major images of the traveler on the psychic quest. In the next passage the narrator claims a universal identity with all levels of consciousness simultaneously ("no one" but all, at once). Images of the three brains—"crocodiles" (reptile), "baboon" (mammal), and "light" (new brain)—

lead up to the identity with the "angel breaking into three parts." This level of consciousness is as close as Bly gets to God, as he punningly suggests in the first line of the passage: "I have floated in the eternity of the cod heaven." The state of "floating" is in Bly one of psychic fullness, harmony, and completion, akin to "flying"; it is the opposite of "fighting" in his poetic lexicon.

"I am a thorn" begins the third and final long catalog of this "joyful chorus." It is a compilation of images looking outward from the individual human psyche and asserting the narrator's brotherhood, even identity, with the protean creative spirit of the universe. It is a résumé of and finale to most of the major motifs of the poem, bringing to them a sense of resolution and reverberation; and it is a tour de force intended not only to express again the multiplicitous, often paradoxical, nature of consciousness ("I am an eternal happiness fighting in long reeds") but also to move beyond it by capturing it in a poetry equal to its protean nature. Understood in these terms, this final section of "An Extra Joyful Chorus" stands as a fully appropriate conclusion to the entire poem "Sleepers Joining Hands." That Bly intended this effect is obvious, since the poem's title occurs in the final line of this section. The narrator's "I" speaks the catalogs, but the poem concludes in the tone of "our":

> Our faces shine with the darkness reflected from the Tigris,
> cells made by the honeybees that go on growing after death,
> a room darkened with curtains made of human hair.
>
> The panther rejoices in the gathering dark.
> Hands rush toward each other through miles of space.
> All the sleepers in the world join hands.

This end is appropriate for the poet's claim to universality, as well as for his appeal to a collective memory ("the darkness reflected from the Tigris") and a shared human nature (in the Jungian sense), two elements necessary to make the claim to universality valid. Finally, the poem suggests a possible immortality through the individual's participation in the genetic wisdom of the collective memory, in the "cells . . . that go on growing after death."

The final three lines of the poem borrow an image from Rilke to express the reconciliation of masculine ("the panther") and feminine ("the gathering dark") in the narrator's achieved state of selfhood.

This reconciliation, this unity of consciousness in the narrator, is then extended outward to embrace other people, humanity, who share in the same inheritance of collective memory. Both space and time are overcome by this shared wisdom, for "sleepers" suggests not only those living who are able to unite their twofold consciousness, but also the dead who merely sleep and are reawakened to life each time another person discovers within himself this living legacy of the past, the collective memory. The affirmation of the last line involves all these dimensions; and it further emphasizes the achievement of both selfhood and collectivity/community through solitude, through the passive meditation of "sleep"—just as did the book's opening "Six Winter Privacy Poems." Bly's political voice of *Light* has finally given way completely to a new voice that combines the public address of his political poetry with a private content made more public by the activity and energy of the inward quest.

There are then, three major aspects to Bly's new voice in *Sleepers*. First, the form of the long poem, consciously declared in the very title of the poem, proves flexible enough to embrace both the central epic quest, with all its dramatic possibilities, and the extensive personal, autobiographical material, with its expository and symbolic developments. Second, centering both dramatic and symbolic personal imagery around the Jungian paradigm of human personality, especially the imagery and concepts of mother consciousness as discussed in the long essay preceding the poem, gives a resonance, a depth to the poetry that makes it more convincing than many of the political poems. Why this should be remains problematical. One might recall Yeats's comment (one Bly himself has used) that when a poet argues with others he makes rhetoric, but when he argues with himself he makes poetry. Third, the push through the Jungian archetype toward a spiritual-religious level of meaning, with accompanying skillful modulations of tone, reveals Bly's coming to grips with problems of belief central not only to himself (as a self-confessed former "Lutheran boy-god") but also to contemporary man—how and what to affirm in an age of disbelief. By making the discovery and the achievement of psychic selfhood lead to an increasing awareness of the existence of God, Bly has created in this long poem a veritable theodicy for the twentieth century. He has justified in contemporary terms—for what could be more current in the twentieth century than psychology?—the existence of evil—here understood as the irrationality of the unconscious life—by showing that it is in fact both necessary and beneficial in man's struggle for full and harmonious participation in the world. The "evil" of the unconscious is within man, but it only appears evil because man, with this century's rationalistic bias, will not acknowledge it or struggle to integrate it into his consciousness. Once again finding in nature the perfect metaphor, Bly expresses beautifully his discovery of the essential unity of a human personality comprised of both conscious and unconscious levels: "For we are like the branch bent in the water . . . / Taken out, it is whole, it was always whole. . . ."

Chapter Five

Nature, Human Nature, and *Gott-Natur:* Robert Bly in the Seventies

The Morning Glory (1975), *This Body Is Made of Camphor and Gopherwood* (1979), *This Tree Will Be Here for a Thousand Years* (1979), and *News of the Universe: Poems of Twofold Consciousness* (1980) represent a coherent grouping of poems, prose poems, and criticism on a common theme, the presence of consciousness in nature. Compared to the political poetry of *Light* and the Jungian poems of *Sleepers,* the work of this period is characterized, as explained in *News,* by the attraction of the poet's imagination to "*Gott-natur,* which means 'divine instinctuality' from one point of view, but also 'non-human nature.' " Bly argues that the poet attracted to this "*Gott-natur* senses the interdependence of all things alive, and longs to bring them all inside a work of art" (*N,* 281). Bly's poetry of this period always expresses his effort to transcend the single consciousness of the rational, human-centered world by discovering and honoring this second, divinely instinctual consciousness in nonhuman nature, this *Gott-natur.* Bly's psyche during this period is engaged in exploring, in learning to see and to live in, a rediscovered universe of what he calls in *News* "twofold consciousness."

The overarching pattern of these four books follows Bly's increasing commitment to two important beliefs. The first is that the world exhibits a consciousness which is different from that which rationalism associates with, and traditionally limits to, human intellect. The second is that he as a poet is writing about man's rediscovery of this other consciousness, and therefore must devise a form suitable for the poetic expression of twofold consciousness. In *News,* whose critical essays present Bly's most thoughtful and extensive statements on these two tenets, he even proclaims the poetry of twofold consciousness as part of a vast but currently neglected literary tradition which, he argues, deserves to be rediscovered. Tracing Bly's development through these three books of poetry, with help from his essays in *News,* will serve to explain the full significance of this period for the poet's career.

The Morning Glory[1] introduces the prose poem, an uncommon hybrid of prose and poetry[2] that Bly was to help make quite popular during the late seventies. Bly declared in *News* that the prose poem was "the final stage of the unpretentious style," especially suitable for allowing the poet's mind to "sink into the mud of earth . . . where the non-human object can live" (*N,* 131–32). In the epigraph to the book, Bly declares his purpose for the switch from poetry to prose poetry. He admires the joy that gradually comes from learning that nature is "independent" of us, "that it has a physical life and a moral life and a spiritual life that is complete without us." Poetry, however free its form, always implies a shaping control of the subject by the poet. But the prose poem form is designed to preserve the independence of the object from the observer, and also to allow for the expression of unpatterned, spontaneous discoveries. In such poetry, as Bly explained in *News,* "the unconscious passes into the object and returns," a union of spirit and perceiving psyche occurs, and the human "unconscious provides material it would not give off if asked directly" (*N,* 213). Thus Bly's prose poem is meant to be a seemingly formless form, designed to express the aleatory, serendipitous quality of the illuminations that the natural world occasionally presents to the psychically attentive observer.

Bly emphasized that the prose poem form was inseparable from his theme of honoring twofold consciousness. In an interview he defined its purpose as a way of breaking out of the "mind-hell" (*T,* 116) characteristic of the contemporary world, a psychic state in which the "organizing mind" controls human perception by habituating people to see the world only in terms of generalities and abstractions, in terms of types rather than the individual, single object. Bly considers the organizing mind's habit of automatically converting individual objects to plurals very dangerous, for it "can control poetry entirely" (*T,* 118) if left unchecked. For Bly, then, "the prose poem is an exercise in moving against 'plural consciousness' " (*T,* 118). It is a form intended to balance modern man's intellectually overdeveloped mind by exposing it to the freshness of the body and the unconscious. Bly's psychospiritual goal, then, determines the prose poem form. In *News,* for instance, he calls these "seeing" poems attempts to heal the "wound" of "city culture" by focusing on one object in nature so intently that the psyche can grant "the whole world its being" (*N*, 250–51).

In *The Morning Glory* Bly presents a range of efforts and experiments with the new prose poem form. Each piece is in prose, of course, but there are a variety of prose poems that test the suitability for the new format of familiar elements of Bly's poetic repertoire. Rapid association, characteristically found in clusters in Bly's leaping poetry, seems too frenetic a motion, and too obviously human-centered, for a prose poem form intent on expressing the consciousness of nature. The concluding sentence of "Looking at a Dry Tumbleweed Brought in from the Snow" proves this. Narratives are sometimes successful, with the plot motion making up for the lack of line and stanza motion, as in "The Hockey Poem" or "Watching Andrei Voznesensky Read in Vancouver." But a narrative parable, "In the Courtyard of the Isleta Mission," fails because it is too self-consciously didactic. A third effort to match old habits with the new form is represented by "Walking on the Sussex Coast," a good poem which is like a *Silence* poem rendered in prose poem form, especially in the steady tone Bly maintains throughout. Catching the proper tone and voice is sometimes a problem for Bly in these early prose poems; he has said that he did not feel the distinctive "pitches"[3] of his speaking voice enter the prose poem until the work of *This Body*. The most successful starts on the prose poem form in part 1 of *The Morning Glory* are "At a Fish Hatchery in Story, Wyoming," "My Three-Year-Old Daughter Brings Me a Gift," and "Standing Under a Cherry Tree at Night." All three of these evince a sharp focus on specific facts of natural objects, with an imaginative development arising organically from nature observed.

In the middle part of *The Morning Glory* are "The Point Reyes Poems," a group published earlier (1974) as a separate book. These are fine poems; as a group they present a consistency of tone, subject, and speaker lacking in the poems of part 1. This may be simply because Bly has found the sea, whose rhythms and formidibility provide a measure for the poet's leaping tendencies. Two of the ten poems attempt to mingle the world of politics with that of nature; "Finding a Salamander on Inverness Ridge" invokes the Vietnam War, and "The Dead Seal at McClure's Beach" speaks of the pollution of the California oil spills. Only the first is in any sense a political poem, and there the comparison between nature and politics does not work, partly because the prose poem form does not support the dialectical tension so crucial to Bly's earlier political poetry.

Part 2's introductory poem, "November Day at McClure's," one of the prose poems which Bly saw fit to include in *News,* makes a striking distinction between the emotions of the human world and nature's instinctuality:

Alone on the jagged rock at the south end of McClure's Beach. The sky low. The sea grows more and more private, as afternoon goes on, the sky comes down closer, the unobserved water rushes out to the horizon, horses galloping in a mountain valley at night. The waves smash up the rock, I find flags of seaweed high on the worn top, forty feet up, thrown up overnight, separated water still pooled there, like the black ducks that fly desolate, forlorn, and joyful over the seething swells, who never "feel pity for themselves," and "do not lie awake weeping for their sins." In their blood cells the vultures coast with furry necks extended, watching over the desert for signs of life to end. It is not our life we need to weep for. Inside us there is some secret. We are following a narrow ledge around a mountain, we are sailing on skeletal eerie craft over the buoyant ocean.

This is an important, early statement of a theme that becomes increasingly important for Bly in the work following *The Morning Glory,* especially in *This Tree* and *Black Coat.* Bly describes the "black ducks that fly desolate, forlorn, and joyful over the seething swells" as magnificent instances of nature's purposeful, instinctual labor. They are aloof from human interpretation, from the pathetic fallacy that Bly here caricatures in quotations imputing human "pity" and human "sin" to the birds. For Bly, like Jung, the pathetic fallacy is a mistake man makes not only about nature but also about himself. Man is not unlike nature; and "inside us there is some secret" which our reason does not see, similar in kind to the divine instinctuality that directs the birds to fly and the ocean to swell. Thus Bly's nature is both similar to and different from human nature, but especially different from mankind's wishes about nature. As in this poem, so in *Black Coat*'s elegy "Mourning Pablo Neruda" Bly refutes the pathetic fallacy so prevalent in an anthropomorphic world, declaring poignantly that dead people whom the living have loved must honor nature's laws "and not come back, / even when we ask them." As a consolation in an elegy, this belief captures the same paradoxical quality of the black ducks flying "desolate, forlorn, and joyful" on nature's

rounds. This fine poem makes a powerful statement of the philosophy
that moved Bly to write in the prose poem form.

An interesting feature of "The Point Reyes Poems" is Bly's increasing ease with his speaking "I." Several of the poems have a flavor of
the diary, with a personal narrator telling anecdotes about, or just
making reference to, his intimate life. In one of the best poems,
"Walking Among Limantour Dunes," Bly begins, "Thinking of a
child soon to be born, I hunch down among the friendly sand
grains." From this personal beginning, Bly moves to a meditation on
the sympathetic correspondences of nature. Similarly, "Climbing up
Mount Vision with My Little Boy" begins as a personal anecdote
("How much I love to feel his small leafy hand curl around my fingers"), though it soon metamorphoses into a pastoral allegory about
father trying to help son climb up Mount Vision. But in these poems,
as well as the final "The Large Starfish," Bly seems more and more
confident in his identity as the speaking "I" of a prose poem, an ob-
servant, curious, more open and less emotional personality than the
"I" of *Sleepers*. If Bly had to wait until *This Body* to find a convincingly personal voice, than he seems to have first begun to identify his
speaker in "The Point Reyes Poems."

The final section of *The Morning Glory* presents several interesting
types of prose poems. "Visiting Thomas Hart Benton and His Wife
in Kansas City" is successful at evoking the scenes and even the brush
strokes of Benton's paintings, and Bly infuses his impressions of Benton with psychological readings of the midwest settlers' psyche. Two
poems on grass, "Walking in the Hardanger Vidda" and "Grass From
Two Years," especially the latter, are skillful interweavings of the
poet's "I" and the natural world. And "A Caterpillar on the Desk,"
in a less emotional vein, does the same thing. "August Rain" endows
the "I" of the earlier family anecdotes with a patriarchal aura, and
looks forward to the poems of *The Man in the Black Coat Turns*.

The two concluding poems, "Christmas Eve Service at Midnight at
St. Michael's" and "Opening the Door of a Barn I Thought Was
Empty on New Year's Eve," are explicitly religious in theme and image, beautiful expressions of the conjunction of the natural world and
the divine instinctuality of *Gott-natur*. The last poem, especially, captures this theme in its description of cows in a barn, with their inherited wisdom from "the instinct reservoir." These creatures possess a
limited consciousness, but one different in degree rather than kind
from that of humans. Using his metaphor of consciousness as light,

Bly characterizes cow consciousness as "too much flesh, the body with the lamp inside, fluttering on a windy night." But rather than expressing a superiority of man to nature, this image unites both man and nature in a continuum of consciousness. Although the cows are "bodies with no St. Theresas," no ecstasy, no "light around the body," still Bly recognizes man's kinship with these beasts and the nature they represent. In important ways, this poem complements the one preceding it, with the priest's sermon "that Christ intended to leave his body behind . . . it is confusing . . . we take our bodies with us when we go." The spiritual theme of these concluding poems of *The Morning Glory* looks forward to the pervasive spirituality of the next book, *This Body*.

This Body Is Made of Camphor and Gopherwood

This Body[4] draws upon imagery that is less directly physical and more metaphysical, even spiritual, then *The Morning Glory*. It is the product of an essentially "religious impulse,"[5] which in its expression occasionally seems bardic and false,[6] but that just as often can be stunningly simple and fine. The book continues the earlier line of development, with perhaps less spontaneous discovery but more sustained, overt praise of the consciousness in nature, the *Gott-natur*. The book's title underscores the sacramental relationship Bly sees between the natural and the spiritual worlds. "Camphor and Gopherwood" are the two woods God told Noah in a dream-vision to use to build the Ark. This boat of salvation is the Old Testament symbol of the special relationship between a divinity who most often manifests himself in natural objects rather than face-to-face and a humanity whose faith enables it to interpret such sacramental epiphanies. For Bly, the body is modern man's ark, a physical creation that is inseparable from the spirit it houses and protects, as he images it in the early poem "The Left Hand." The human body, through the divine instinctuality that characterizes its consciousness, is man's link to the *Gott-natur* infusing the entire universe.

As the title suggests, this is Bly's book of the holiness of the body. As the book progresses, the body becomes a metonymy for the divine instinctuality that animates not only all of nature but also the spirit of man and the art he creates. In the first poem, "Walking Swiftly," this energy begins as "heat inside the human body," then is transformed in stages into mankind's highest achievement, powering "the artist [who] walks swiftly to his studio, and carves oceanic waves into the dragon's mane." In "Snowed In" Bly again equates the energy in nature with that in art, proclaiming they "are both the same flow, that starts out close to the soil" but grows and manifests itself in different ways: it "is at home when one or two are present, . . . and in the burnt bone that sketched the elk by smokey light" in the ancient caves of Lascaux.

If the body's energy can transform itself into art, it can also establish links in various ways between man and nature, a basis of correspondence between the two. Several poems treat this theme of correspondence from different angles. "Looking from Inside My Body" compares the conscious and unconscious regions of human personality to sun and moon, and the body to "earth . . . earth things, earthly joined." At night the sun-consciousness "will drop underneath the earth, and travel sizzling along the underneath-ocean-darkness path," the inward road of psychic exploration, which is Bly's major poetic symbol. In this extended correspondence, the significant thing is that the body does not break the circuit the way the rationalists always say it must; in fact, the body consciousness, what Bly in *News* terms "night intelligence" (*N*, 1) provides the most important part of the road to self-knowledge which man must travel.

In "Falling Into Holes in Our Sentences" the body is presented both as a corrective to the spirit, protecting it, but also as a continually changing manifestation of the psyche. It is a "ruthless body performing its magic, transforming each of our confrontations into energy." This body continually creates correspondence between psychic and somatic phenomena. It continually teaches man of the inescapable relationship between body and soul, even by compensating such persona behavior as lecturing "about the confusion of others" by sending a subconscious impulse to accidentally drive the car "off the road."

Another bodily basis of correspondence between man and nature is their shared evolutionary history. In "Coming in For Supper" Bly presents a very specific instance of an ancient ritual, having supper with the family. He locates the power of the occasion in its long psychic history, in "those long dusks—they were a thousand years long then—that fell over the valley from the cave mouth (where we sit)." The poet emphasizes how so much of human evolutionary history was based on learning (slowly) from nature, as in his lament for "the last man killed by flu who knew how to weave a pot of river clay the way the wasps do . . . Now he is dead and only the wasps know in the long river-mud grief." Similarly, in "Snowed In" Bly emphasizes the continuum linking nature to man, based on their shared evolutionary heritage, of the divine instinctuality of *Gott-natur*. A man and a woman are snowed in, but "in the snow storm millions of years come close behind us, nothing is lost, nothing rejected, our bodies are equal to the snow in energy," and ready to affirm themselves again.

"The Origin of the Praise of God" deals most fully with the religious aspect of the body and its *Gott-natur* energy. This poem is placed at the center of the book, and accompanied, as each poem is, by a drawing of a snail that presents a frontal view of the creature's cornucopian trumpet, as if to announce and amplify the importance of the poem. Further, this poem is the only one of the book Bly included in his anthology *News of the Universe,* which is a measure of its significance to his theory of consciousness as well as a testament to its worth as poetry. In this poem Bly brings together the major themes of *This Body.* The presence of a consciousness, a wisdom, in nature, one which man would do well to honor and learn from, is a pervasive theme, emphasized again and again simply by an imagery that consistently represents human energy at the cellular level as indistinguishable from the energy of all living things. At the poem's beginning Bly declares this equivalence, "this body is made of bone and excited protozoa . . . and it is with my body that I love the fields." At the poem's conclusion he repeats this correspondence, and emphasizes as well the divine instinctuality of both nature's and man's fundamental, cellular energies, affirming that "from the dance of the cells praise sentences rise to the throat of the man."

The holiness of the body, and the psychospiritual nature of the human imperative to pursue the inward road of self-exploration, are two major themes of Bly's work, and both are expressed more forcefully in this poem than in any other in the book. Bly's answer to the question implied by the poem's title is that the origin of the praise of God lies in the inescapable impulse of life's most ancient and enduring energies operating at the cellular level. This impulse is nature's evolutionary imperative to increase and multiply, to create new life. Behind the human emotions of two lovers lies the force of millions of years of evolutionary history, urging man at the instinctual level to once again re-create himself. When two people approach each other,

then beneath ego consciousness and even beneath the stimulation felt
through the five senses, an exchange takes place:

So the space between two people diminishes, it grows less and less, no one
to weep, they merge at last. The sound that pours from the fingertips awakens clouds of cells far inside the body, and beings unknown to us start out
in a pilgrimage to their Saviour, to their holy place. Their holy place is a
small black stone, that they remember from Protozoic times, when it was
rolled away from a door . . . and it was after that they found their friends,
who helped them to digest the hard grains of this world. . . . The cloud of
cells awakens, intensifies, swarms . . . the cells dance inside beams of sun-
light so thin we cannot see them. . . . To them each ray is a vast palace,
with thousands of rooms. From the dance of the cells praise sentences rise to
the throat of the man praying and singing alone in his room. He lets his
arms climb above his head, and says, "Now do you still say you cannot
choose the Road?"

As the poem progresses, the poet resorts to overtly religious imagery to express the strength and significance of this *Gott-natur* impulse
that moves man. Bly draws on the imagery of the Resurrection of Jesus, perhaps the most potent belief in the Christian tradition, to express the urge humans feel to honor the *Gott-natur* by procreating. In
Bly's image, the myth of resurrection is powerful precisely because it
symbolically reenacts the archetypal event of procreation, whose
memory man has carried in the collective unconscious "from Protozoic
times." Thus Bly images the journey of the sperm toward the womb
as a "pilgrimage" to "the holy place." And a successful impregnation
is described as a stone "rolled away from a door," an image taken directly from the biblical account of Christ's Resurrection, where the
angel rolled away the stone blocking the sepulcher of Christ.

The poem concludes by describing how this archetypal, *Gott-natur*
urge leads to the imperative to "choose the Road," the inward path
of psychospiritual exploration. Not only the religious imagery of the
last half of the poem, but also the situations at the poem's end of
"the man praying and singing," affirming with his whole body,
"from the dance of the cells" to the "praise sentences" of his voice,
the archetypal "Road," underscores Bly's belief in the essentially religious nature of a body "made of camphor and gopherwood."

This Tree Will Be Here for a Thousand Years

This book of forty-four poems consists of two parts. The first twenty poems were originally published in 1975 as *Old Man Rubbing His Eyes*,[7] and the remainder were added in 1979. Yet in the introductory essay, "The Two Presences," Bly says that *This Tree* includes all the poems written in the style of his first book, *Silence,* since its publication in 1962, and that affinities of style and subject make his latest book seem like a continuation of the first. Bly's desire to compare his latest work to his first, nearly twenty years older, tells less about the two books than it does about an impulse in the poet that the reader senses in the poetry of *This Tree,* the impulse of a survivor to affirm continuity and order in a world which in human terms is breaking apart. The book's title emphasizes survival and endurance, imaging a pine tree that can grow in terrain where a leafy tree would die, a pine tree that can find its place and stay "for a thousand years." Further, Bly's pine tree symbolizes the mood of a poet growing older, not only strong and long-lived but also "somber, / made for winter, they knew it would come" (*Tr,* 36).

In this book Bly emphasizes a new aspect of the *Gott-natur,* not merely its divine instinctuality but also its profound, even sorrowful fidelity to nature's eternal laws. The poet is neither the curious observer of *The Morning Glory* nor the passionate believer of *This Body.* Rather he is a human who has been through what in "Women We Never See Again" Bly calls the "human war." Consequently, he seeks to infuse in the poetry a psychic weight gained from his newly heightened sense of human frailty. In his essay "The Image as a Form of Intelligence" Bly identified this quality of "psychic weight" as one of the six sources of power in poetry, as significant as imagery or sound or story. He declares that this quality is directly connected to the poet's life and experience, "to grief, turning your face to your own life, absorbing the failures your parents and your own country have suffered."[8] In *This Body* the new tone, and a deeper resonance, comes from Bly's balancing this psychic weight with a deepened appreciation of nonhuman nature's consciousness of eternity, by focusing on what he once referred to as "the old non-human or non-ego energies the ancients imagined so well" (*N,* 80). Much of Bly's effort in *This Tree* is skillfully directed to merging the psychic weight of his own life and the eternal laws of the *Gott-natur,* for the purpose of affirming

a relationship between the individual and the eternal that might endure beyond his lifetime. As he says in his essay in the image as intelligence, "when a poet creates a true image, he is gaining knowledge;
he is bringing up into consciousness a connection that has been forgotten, perhaps for centuries."[9] Later, in *Black Coat,* Bly puts more
emphasis on the dialectical relationship between the psychic weight
of personal experience and the general laws of nature, to show that
man must live his life between the two, that this is what it means to
be human in a *Gott-natur* world. Nevertheless, the poems in *This Tree*
and even *Black Coat* are intended not only to evince the melancholy
tone of psychic weight gained from the poet's personal experience,
but also to affirm Bly's metaphysics concerning the interdependence
between the individual and the natural laws that sustain him. Bly is
writing about much more here than merely the difficulty of his personal life.

Bly's belief that man and nature can "share a consciousness" (*Tr,*
9) is the subject of his introductory essay to *This Tree.* He contrasts
human consciousness, "insecure, anxious, massive, earthbound, persistent, cunning, hopeful," and nature's nonhuman consciousness,
which not only lacks these qualities but also continually frustrates
man's desire to impose human emotions on it, to subordinate its true
presence to human wishes about its presence. Bly does see in organic
nature a thanatos instinct, an awareness of death, "a melancholy tone,
the tear inside the stone, what Lucretius calls 'the tears of things,' an
energy circling downward, felt often in autumn" (*Tr,* 9–10). Indeed,
this melancholy tone humming through the nature of things is the
dominant one in part 1 of *This Tree.* As Bly explains in *News,* "each
time a human being's desire-energy leaves his body, and goes out into
the hills or forest, the desire-energy whispers to the ear as it leaves:
'You know, one day you will die.' " Bly calls this whisper evidence
that the two consciousnesses "have spoken to each other," and argues
that it is good for humans to hear nature's whisper of death, for "it
helps the human to come down, to be on the ground" (*N,* 281) and
to locate human consciousness in relationship to nature's consciousness.

A further aspect of the *Gott-natur* emphasized in *This Tree* is its
primitive, "non-human instinctuality" (*N,* 281), the energy that
drives the universe. A powerful expression of this occurs in the introductory poem of part 2 of the book: "Sometimes when you put your
hand into a hollow tree / you touch the dark places between the

stars." This is a Lawrentian image of the discovery of the palpable presence of the nothingness and the magnitude of infinity and eternity, measured against which all human calculations and ego-emotions pale. Bly once paraphrased Lawrence as saying that "when you look up, in most centuries, you do not see the black sky with the stars," but a humanized version, a painted unbrella, because "humanity prefers that, it is less scary." But "a strong artist will tear holes in the umbrella so you can see the stars again." Bly added, "I like Lawrence's image—it explains a lot to me" (*T*, 255–56). *This Tree* is Bly's conscious attempt to tear holes in the umbrella. Another expression of this sentiment comes from Wallace Stevens's "The Snow Man," selected by Bly for *News*. Stevens declares that man "must have a mind of winter," must look at the world and behold "Nothing that is not there and the nothing that is." *This Tree* provides examples of both.

Part 1 develops two associated themes, death and the breakdown of family relationships. The movement of part 1 is from fall to winter, with a final, coda poem about the psyche of winter existing even in the midst of summer, which underscores Bly's winter as a psychic state, a season of the soul. The theme of death is present from beginning to end. "Writing Again" is a dismissal of the moralistic poetry of Bly's Vietnam period as unsuitable to his present imagination, a passionate exercise that does not answer the question of the poem's conclusion, "what good will it do me in the grave?" Death and eternity are to be the measures of life's acts. Similarly, "Fall Poem" dismisses the ecstatic religious moods of *This Body* as insufficient to his present need. Bly defines the season as one of promise forever unfulfilled: "Something is about to happen! / Christ will return! / But each fall it goes by without happening." In "Dawn in Threshing Time" the rebirth of the day is not enough to lighten the burden of death the poet feels, which he admits he has felt evey morning "after thirty," the realization that "he is not strong enough to die." The image of the cradle as well as the rhythm of the last line recall Whitman's famous poem about a similar discovery, "Out of the Cradle Endlessly Rocking." "To Live" repeats this paradox, that the more a man lives, the closer he gets to death, for "To live is to rush ahead eating up your own death." "Listening to a Cricket in the Wainscoting" is a better poem, finding four surreal image equivalents for the cricket's chirp, all of which invoke blackness and death.

"A Long Walk Before the Snows Began" uses Bly's ubiquitous image of snow to suggest the threat of death. In this poem Bly's walk takes him to the recognition that "It must be that I will die one day!" This leads to a vision of himself as dead, in which "I see my body lying stretched out. / A woman whose face I cannot see stands near my body." There is nothing in the poem that suggests resurrection or hope of any sort. Similarly, in "Roads" Bly creates a four-line elegy, dedicated "In memoriam" to someone unnamed, which only hints at a possible consolation in the image of "the plowing west" that reminds the grieving poet of natural resurrections, of "mountain tops, or the chest of graves." The mood of the poet after the elegy is one of extreme vulnerability. In "Passing An Orchard By Train," the concluding poem of part 1, the season is summer, but the mood is dead-of-winter. The poet declares that "We cannot bear disaster" as nature seems to; as humans, "One slight bruise and we die!" The poet is repelled from nature, back to his fellowman, for comfort; even a stranger on the train, because he is human-kind, is better than this melancholy isolation, which Bly had so often praised in the past as solitude. If Bly is the "old man rubbing his eyes" of the original title, then his tears signify a need for community, for human forgiveness, as the book's first part concludes.

The second theme, the breakdown of family relationships, is entwined with the theme of death. Bly's avowed intention to write a poetry that mingles hints of the poet's personal life amid more impersonal, cosmic themes, in order to evoke the shared consciousness, the interrelationship, between the two worlds, is evident in several poems. "Sitting in Fall Grass" opens with the poet hearing the voices of the cosmos, of wind, ocean, and sun; but in the final stanza the poet is attuned to different voices, speaking of separation and differences, saying "I am not like you . . . / I must live so." In "Thinking of 'Seclusion' " Bly imagines living without family responsibilities. He awakens on a day when there is no work to be done, when even his self-imposed task of writing "looks small beside the growing trees." He fantasizes, jokingly, about what a permanent "seclusion" might mean, no worries about the children, leaving the money problems to the wife, living "your whole life like a drunkard's dream!" The poem presents an unresolved tension between the two worlds, the human and the cosmic; but there is also a sense of shared consciousness, in which the human world seems akin to, even interdependent with, the natural world. Both worlds are part of a farm that to Bly "looks doubly good."

"Digging Worms" expresses more directly Bly's association of the themes of death and the breakdown of the family. The poet is "digging worms behind the chickenhouse," an act of penance as well as self-examination. In stanza 2 he reflects on the relationship between parents and children, a paradoxical one of mutual support and burden. Like tightwire walkers carrying each other, staggering, "along a wire our children balance us / on their shoulders, we balance their graves / on ours." In stanza 3 Bly images the unraveling of family relationships, not only between parents and children but also between husband and wife, in "we unwind / from some kind of cocoon made by lovers . . . until / with one lurch we grow still and look down at our shoes." The poem concludes with a dream of insignificant acts of carelessness adding up until they pull down a "castle," the poet's home.

Part 2 of the book is different in tone from part 1, because it presents not only poems contrasting the different consciousnesses of nature and man, but also poems expressing their shared consciousness, in which Bly finds a source of consolation. The first poem, "Women We Never See Again," sets the tone by imaging time's infinity and space's immensity as "the dark spaces between the stars." Nature's immensity is both impervious and inviting to human consciousness, a "fortress made of ecstatic blue stone," an edifice bespeaking a second consciousness to which inhabitants of the human world may aspire, by which they may measure their human actions. In "Amazed By an Accumulation of Snow" Bly writes of another manifestation of nature's consciousness of the immensity of the universe. This is a "call" poem, described in *News* as a poem about an instance when "one form of consciousness [calls] to another" (*N*, 35). The last stanza cites several forms of the call, ending with "The horse's hoof kicks up a seashell, and the farmer / finds an Indian stone with a hole all the way through." In similar fashion, Bly draws correspondances in "Pulling a Rowboat Up Among Lake Reeds" between the two presences by associating the darkness of nature and of the human world, including birth and religious sacrifice.

An important way in which Bly emphasizes the difference between the two presences in part 2 is by intentionally demystifying nature, by rendering it impervious to man's tendency to project human emotions upon it. Bly critiques the anthropomorphism of the pathetic fallacy in a series of poems in which he presents nature as not responding to or bearing messages for the ego-centered human, but instead constantly affirming what Bly described in *News* as "news of the universe" (*N*, 281). In "July Morning" Bly begins with a blithe description of nature communing with itself, personified, talking to man—in short, a perfect expression of the pathetic fallacy. A morning dove even "coos" to his audience "a cathedral, / then the two arms of the cross!" But Bly undercuts this falsely romantic view of nature on a July morning by looking beyond the moment, by invoking the laws of time that govern organic nature: the same evocative magic which creates the "rabbit/hopping along the garden" also creates the rabbit's death. Laconically, like Emily Dickinson, Bly ends the poem thus: "After that we will be alone in the deep blue reaches of the river" of time, without the rabbit or a blind faith in July mornings.

In the following poem, "An Empty Place," Bly achieves a similar Dickinsonian irony by contrasting the joyful attitude toward nature in the introductory, prose poem stanza with the concluding stanza of poetry. The initial situation of a speaker affirming "a joy in emptiness" because each space offers "a place to live" ultimately gives way to a tone of uncertainty and perhaps even bitterness. The speaker wonders at "a white chicken's feather that still seems excited by the warm blood" now gone forever, and he looks upon an empty corncob, lacking all its kernels, as a "place of many mansions, / which Christ has gone to prepare for us." There is little succor in such a line, uttered by the same poet who wrote in "Fall Poem" of the failure of Christ to fulfill his promise to return. Instead, this poem, like "Prayer Service in an English Church," is precisely about the failure of nature to support human hopes in the orthodox religious terms in which they are so often cast.

Nature's denial of conventional religious interpretations of it forces the poet to break with his socially inculcated habits of looking at it, especially strong in one who was raised as a "Lutheran Boy-god in Minnesota,"[10] and to see nature in a new way. "Fishing on a Lake at Night" represents a turning point in part 2, where the poet is able to accept without despair the elements and consciousness of nature as independent of conventional religious interpretation. Further, this poem expresses Bly's description in *News* of consciousness in nature as being "not exactly consciousness, nor psyche, nor intelligence, nor sentience," but mainly characterized by elemental "energy" (*N*, 286–87). This energy of nature's consciousness need not be exuberant, like the flying around associated with the ecstatic body. Light, grass, and snow are elemental energies in Bly's poetry.

The poem begins by subverting the conventional religious image of God as man's guiding light. Here the light is an element of nature that "simply comes," carrying no messages from the supernatural, "bearing no gifts, / as if the camels had arrived without the Wise Men." But it offers another kind of solace, for it "is steady, holding us to our old mountain home," to the ancient sense of human sharing in the *Gott-natur* of the universe. The moon, too, "arrives without a fuss," but without promises. It is similarly demystified of supernatural portent; for its light "goes between the boards around the pulp-cutter's house— / the same fence we pass through by opening the gate."

Part 2 of *This Tree,* unlike part 1, moves through despair to hope. The concluding twelve poems emphasize the magnitude of nature and the necessity that human consciousness learn to locate itself within this larger context. In "Night of First Snow" the poet envisions man as an assertive "dark vertical shape to the earth." In the final two stanzas he can distinguish the two presences, identifying the human and individual aspect of nature's eternal, repetitive laws. "Solitude of the Two Day Snowstorm" similarly locates the "frail impulses" of the human, including the family, within the context of nature's immense forces, symbolized by the snowstorm. But a black crow's head, not only nature's handiwork but also a totem of human consciousness, looking "intense, swift, decided," asserts itself against the all-blanketing snow.

But the melancholy tone remains an important counterpoint during the final poems of part 2. In "Frost in the Ground" it is the poet's recognition that "what I have / to say I have not said." In "Late Moon" it is the dying light over his father's farm, "in the west that eats it away." A similar theme of nature's laws of time and death occurs in "Black Pony Eating Grass," where the poet marvels that "In a few years we will die, / yet the grass continues to lift itself into the horse's teeth." Nature continues living in spite of the inevitability of death—both man and the stars are "stubborn" in their urge to live. This paradox is imaged in "Nailing a Dock Together," where "the horse stands penned, but is also free. / It is a horse whose neck human / beings have longed to touch for centuries," ever since man's rationalism created a gap between man and nature. The horse symbolizes the *Gott-natur,* the divine instinctuality of nature's persistent energy, which can prove an effective antidote to excessive human melancholy about dying.

This Tree concludes with two poems emphasizing the magnitude of nature as well as the possibility of humans sharing consciousness with

nature. "An Evening When the Full Moon Rose as the Sun Set" celebrates a visual balance of the two natural forces that govern the world,
moon, and sun, which symbolize for Bly nature's nonrational consciousness and man's rational consciousness. The event for Bly, and
the poem for the reader, exemplify perfectly a moment and a poetry,
as praised in *News,* when "the ancient union of the day intelligence of
the human being and the night intelligence of nature become audible,
palpable again" (*N,* 4). The poem is a vision of a world under the
spell of *Gott-natur,* living "the life of faithfulness," a term underscor-
ing the psychoreligious satisfaction derived from fidelity to nature's
archaic forces.

The final poem of *This Tree,* "Out Picking Up Corn," is about the
poet's learning to find food in pastures "eaten clean by horse teeth,"
learning to get nourishment from sources "respectable people do not
want to take in." This latter statement could almost serve as a sum-
mary of Bly's literary career. But Bly is not desolate, but hopeful. As
he did at the conclusion of "Sleepers Joining Hands," here Bly turns
to an admixture of religious language and parable to express his new
state of mind. He declares, "Surely we do not eat only with our
mouths, / or drink only by lifting our hands!" He presents in quotations a Zen-like utterance of a disciple, "My master has gone picking
ferns on the mountain." The final image of "walking in fog near the
cliff" expresses the poet's sense of himself as older, closer to death,
lacking a clear vision of what lies at the end of his road, yet nourished
and heartened by the very atmosphere in which he walks. Water has
always been a symbol used by Bly to suggest nourishment of the conscious life by the unconscious, as in his elegy for Pablo Neruda. Here
the damp fog quenches the poet's thirst through osmosis, as the *Gott-*
natur nourishes the human consciousness, just as Bly described it in
the book's introductory essay on the beneficial interdependence of the
two presences.

News of the Universe:
Poems of Twofold Consciousness

In 1980 Robert Bly published *News,* an extensive poetry anthology
accompanied by critical essays that are often directly applicable to
Bly's own poetry of this period. In *News* Bly argued for nothing less
than a new version of Western literary and intellectual history. His
poetry selections were chosen to illustrate a tradition that champions
the possibility of humanity's achieving "twofold consciousness,"

which Bly defines as awareness of unity not only within the human psyche, between conscious and unconscious aspects, but also between "the human psyche and nature" (*N*, 5). The fundamental message this literary tradition of twofold consciousness communicates to its audience is "news of the universe," and this news is that man can gain a sense of the possibility of inner, psychic unity by learning to see an external unity in nature.

News begins by briefly tracing the tradition's subjugation by eighteenth-century rationalism, and continues with a fuller treatment of the counterattack led by Blake in England and the continental romantics Goethe, Holderlin, and Novalis. The largest portion of the anthology deals with the tradition's struggle in the early twentieth century to prevail against the neoclassicism of the Pound-Eliot tradition, as well as with the literature of twofold consciousness's emergence since 1945 as the dominant tradition. Bly defines the major tradition of modernism as the "lineage of double consciousness, or 'full consciousness' " (*N*, 84). Bly's book even infers the tradition's future from the poetry of other cultures, such as the Eskimo, which seem to have arrived at a unity of consciousness before Western civilization.

Throughout this chapter the essays and even the poetry of *News* have shed light on Bly's own efforts to write poetry that brings news of the universe and of a rediscovered nature. But his anthology speaks also to concerns that span his entire career. *News* raises such perennial subjects as Bly's anti-academic stance (imagine this history as opposed to that commonly assigned textbook, the Norton anthology). Also, this literary history argues for Bly's anti-rational epistemology, praising a kind of poetry devoted to exploring beyond the rationalist conception of consciousness, seeking news of the universe rather than "news of the human mind" (*N*, 281). Finally, the book is a virtual catalog of Bly's acknowledged influences: the European romantics Goethe, Novalis, Blake, and Rilke; non-Western poets such as Kabir, Basho, and some Amerind artists; and, of course, the Spanish surrealists Lorca, Jiminez, and Neruda. Bly himself has translated[11] most of these poets. Many of these writers were either unappreciated or unknown to most American academics and poets twenty-five years ago; this anthology is a reminder that it is Bly who is mainly responsible for their general acceptance today. *News,* then, is indispensible as Bly's own textbook on himself, not only on his efforts to rediscover nature during this period, but also on many of the major themes and sources that inform his entire career.

Chapter Six

The Family of Man, Imagined: *The Man in the Black Coat Turns*

Bly's poetry in the seventies dealt primarily with the consciousness of nature and the correspondences man discovers between nature and himself. But *The Man in the Black Coat Turns*[1] displays Bly's increased identification with human relationships, both in his personal family and in the evolutionary family of man. Though the seventies' theme of an ineluctable correspondence between man and nature remains important, *Black Coat* marks a significant turning in Bly's career. For the first time the poet systematically draws upon material from his most intimate relationships—husband, father, and son—seeking to discover and to affirm the possibilities for freedom and creative human behavior available within *This Tree*'s vision of the deterministic laws of the universe. The interdependence of humans in a family is the new region of the psyche to which Bly's inward road now leads him, a region he feels he must explore and assimilate if his lifelong task of what Jung described as individuation and integration is to proceed. In *Black Coat*, then, Bly's new subject is this family of man, especially as it is explored, shaped, and preserved by the poet's imagination. This new subject supplants the private, phenemenological world of *Silence*, the psychopolitical world of *Light*, the Jungian dreamscape of *Sleepers*, and the psychoreligious landscape of *The Morning Glory* and *This Tree*.

During the previous decade Bly's family underwent great changes. His brother died, his children grew, his father grew older, his early friend James Wright died, as did his mentor Pablo Neruda, and Bly divorced and remarried, becoming the overfifty father in a blended family. These events all find their way into Bly's work, either through specific allusion or the black coloration of human mutability and grief influencing Bly's poetry from *The Point Reyes Poems* through

Black Coat. Nevertheless, Bly the artist always moves beyond the personal aspect of his grief to an encounter with universal themes, whether human nature or human family, especially in terms of the overall development of his books. Bly's poems in *Black Coat,* then, present the family of man in its broadest aspects—not only the relationship between husband, wife, and children, but also between generations, especially fathers and sons, as well as more distant ancestors, both remembered and forgotten, who make up the evolutionary human tree. Thus at the book's conclusion, Bly's symbolic association of the poet with a Christ-Odin figure, and consequently the poet's family with the entire human race redeemed through poetic imagination, seems neither unprepared for nor unjustified.

Black Coat's increasing emphasis on the role of the artist in affirming the human family and redeeming it from the oblivion of time is an important new theme in Bly's work. The poetic style in *Black Coat* seems to reflect Bly's greater concern for the community of poets and their common craft; Bly admits to becoming more aware of such traditional strengths of poetry as tone, resonating interior sound, and story, which Bly includes among the six powers of poetry in his essay "Recognizing the Image." He is also more interested in identifying himself through *Black Coat's* many allusions and imitations (Whitman, Dickinson, Neruda, Auden, Eberhart, Yeats, Faulkner, and others) as a poet working within a poetic tradition. Most importantly, he preaches what he practices, elevating poetic labor and craft to a theme in this book, and giving it an important role in his new vision of the possibilities of human affirmation in a world which, to the aging poet, seems more and more constrained by fate and the laws of nature. It is certainly no accident that a book emphasizing the importance of the human poetic imagination in redeeming the family of man from nature's fate of death and inevitable oblivion should turn for an appropriate symbol of the poet-shaman to the Norse god Odin, whose crucifixionlike self-sacrifice won for mankind the "runes," hidden words redeemed from beyond, and therefore to some degree sharing the power of, death.

Bly's arrangement of the book's three parts enforces his sense of dialectical opposition leading to resolution and even affirmation. Part 1 declares the poet's felt sense of the powerful forces of determinism—in nature, in society, and in the individual personality—which seem to deny any possibility of human freedom or growth. Part 2 uses the more tentative prose poem form to describe the poet's assays of the hard problems posed in part 1; in the second part, nature's laws, which seemed so inscrutable and forbidding in part 1, become under consideration more comprehensible, even purposeful, and occasionally wondrous, as in "A Bouquet of Roses." Part 3 presents twelve poems, some of them among Bly's best, that seek to reconcile the conflict between nature's determinism and human freedom. Bly affirms man's power to unify his own dialectical, twofold psyche in a conscious act of self-sacrifice; in *Black Coat* Bly cites as examples such acts as a father's playing attentively with a son, a son's honoring his father, and a poet's writing a poem. The labor of the poet, especially, has the potential to affirm not only the artist's individual psyche, but also the consciousness of the race, of the family of man. Yeats's injunction to poets in "Under Ben Bulben" to "bring the soul of man to God / make him fill the cradles right" is very close to Bly's message in "Words Rising" and "Crazy Carlson's Meadow." Both the individual and the human race may thereby partially transcend nature's determinism and death, as in the book's final poem, "Kneeling Down to Look In a Culvert."

Parts 1–2

The autobiographical impulse of Bly's essay on his childhood, "Being a Lutheran Boy-god in Minnesota"[2] hovers over the poems of *Black Coat,* which is dedicated to Bly's son Noah, especially those of parts 1–2. However, the origin of the poet's impulse to reinvent his family past is less historical than psychological, and the record he presents is consequently less important for its biographical facts, even for his personal interpretation of them, than for its simple existence as proof of Bly's psychic urge to explore consciously the nature of a man's identity as a son and as a father. Indeed, Bly has led numerous workshops on the psychological relationships of fathers and sons.[3] Bly's vision of his father must be also partially a vision of himself as a father, so that the "man in the black coat" of the essay and the poems is a figure built upon not only Bly's father but also Bly himself, and ultimately upon the archetypal expectations sons have of fathers, and vice versa, which are stored in the collective human memory.

The essay establishes the importance for Bly of parents in determining their children's psychic life, and presents an unabashedly impressionistic vision of Bly's childhood. His mother chose him, over his older brother James, to be the "favorite son" (*G*, 109), which Bly claims as the cause of his becoming a "boy-god." Bly remembers/imagines his father "wearing a large black coat . . . holding a baby up over the snow; it is my brother or myself" (*G*, 205); the poet symbolizes his father as an imposing figure whose "silence . . . did not bring him more company, but did help carry the burdens higher up the mountain" (*G*, 207). Both these powerful, but ambivalent, images find their way into *Black Coat*. And Bly's essay makes this imagined nuclear family the controlling center of the ever-widening gyres of contemporary society, family ancestors, the evolution of the species, and nature's universal laws.

Bly's melange of styles in the essay, including prose poems, diary, exposition, and parable, also underscores the importance of the poet's imagination in exploring and configuring anew the record of the past, so that it might be transmitted to Bly's children and beyond. By consistently pushing through the personal anecdote to the more universal psychic truth, Bly declares that neither his essay nor the poems of *Black Coat* are best understood as factual recollections of Bly's real, idiosyncratic family. Rather, both essay and poems present a family enlarged by the human imagination, consciously refigured out of bits of fact and memory to satisfy the archetypal urge the individual human has to identify himself as a member of the family of man.

The book's first poem, "Snowbanks North of the House," presents a catalog of natural and social actions that seem governed by unseen, unexplained forces. Bly appeals to common experience: why does a snowbank "stop suddenly six feet from the house"; isn't it true that people can change permanently in one moment—"the wife looks at her husband one night at a party, and loves him no more." This list of ordinary, family events is imbued with extraordinary significance, as in a parable. It concludes when "the man in the black coat turns and goes back down the hill." This archetypal figure/force, perhaps linking the force of nature with the authority of the father in the family, is unexplained and unpredictable. He appears with the finality of doom itself, then with equal inscrutability "pivots / in the dust."

"For My Son Noah, Ten Years Old" is a lesson about the possibilities of growth and freedom within the limits of the human condition. Bly begins by acknowledging the inevitability of nature's processes, especially aging; yet he cites also the endurance of "the old tree" and "the barn" as advocates of "darkness and night," calling to the poet. Bly further qualifies the organic determinism of time-governed nature, its instinct for death, by presenting the barnyard images of nature's counter-instinct, its life-instinct to change and evolve: the horse turns its body," the chicken urges its nearly useless wings to fly it up to a roost. Man, too, a "kind" to these "primitive" animals, "slowly" reconciles the conflict of his own dual nature and of his family, "comes closer, loses his rage, sits down at table."

The poem concludes by applying the lesson of nature to Bly's family life. The father is proud, not only of his son but also of his role of father, watching his progeny evolve through the stages of human life. Significantly, Bly calls these times of "undivided" tenderness, with the fragmentation within the psyche and within the family reconciled because each person perceives himself and the others as members of the family of man.

"The Prodigal Son" presents the archetypal family struggle of the father-son relationship, "father beyond father beyond father," as typical also of the dialectic between human consciousness and nature's laws. To be human is to struggle consciously to assert individuality against unconscious forces, whether nature, family structure, or human ignorance. As Bly was to write later, "What can we do but choose? The only way for human beings / is to choose."[4] But being human also involves learning to accept one's place in the order of nature. Bly's allusion to the biblical Prodigal Son parable not only invokes the psychoreligious lessons of family acceptance and forgiveness, but also establishes a firm correspondence between modern family dynamics and inherited, archetypal patterns. In this poem the Prodigal Son's struggle to submit to his father's authority is similar to his father's struggle to submit to nature's laws by accepting the inevitability of his own death. Bly's image for both is "bending the head, looking into the water," discovering that "Under the water there's a door." This symbolic threshold can be a passage between states of consciousness, between sons becoming fathers, and perhaps even between death and life after death. This image foreshadows the crucial image of the ever-renewing lake in the final poem of the book.

Bly concludes part 1 by subtly affirming the continuity of the family of poets, a theme that becomes more prominent as *Black Coat* progresses. "Mourning Pablo Neruda" is a beautifully understated elegy for the great Chilean writer, one of Bly's acknowledged poetic fathers. Similar in this and other respects to Auden's "In Memory of W. B. Yeats," Bly's elegy is also about what poetry can and cannot do. Bly compares Neruda and his poetry to water: life-giving, ubiquitous, indomitable. Water, like Neruda, gives naturally, without intending anything to happen; its strength comes from obeying nature's laws, flowing on "to where / it has to be." The poem ends declaring that there is no point in building a monument or laying flowers on Neruda's grave, for, like water, the poet in his poetry is simultaneously everywhere and "gone." Neruda is mentioned only in the poem's title, and a controlled understatement of the speaker's grief, aided by a terse poetic line, emphasizes the poem's emotion. The speaker's assurance of Neruda's immortality, a conclusion traditional to the elegy, is only hinted at by associating Neruda's life with water's cyclical life-death-resurrection. But Bly does accept a son's traditional role as vessel for the father, for he imagines this elegy while driving to the country shack where he writes his poetry, carrying in his car the jar of drinking water that inspired the elegaic comparison.

Part 2 of *Black Coat* evinces some development through its six prose poems. The first two present fate, and fatalism, as forces that can sometimes overwhelm man's sense of his own freedom. The second two discover in nature correspondences for the human condition that inspire the poet with hope and joy, even in darkness. The final poems invoke the family of poets and the work of poetry to hint at possible ways to redeem human consciousness from the oblivion that befalls the natural world. In part 2 the subject of the relationship between son and father broadens to include all family relationships and generationality. The color black, darkness, and the grave still pervade the imagistic tapestry, but the inexorable finality of nature and fate is leavened by the suggestions of intent and purpose in nature's movement. The possibilities of man's turning and overcoming such an environment begin to emerge, and they are identified by the poet as man's heritage and the artist's justification.

"Eleven O'Clock at Night" presents an intentionally weary, uninspired catalog of the things the poet "cannot escape from" through writing poetry, including the quotidian routine, his lethargic body, society's rationalistic bias, and, finally, time itself, the "winter dark of late December." His tone changes from personal frustration to philosophical resignation. At the end, he acknowledges that both bad and good come to him whether or not he asks; and in his aging he has come to "long for what I cannot escape from," forces for which "there is no solution."

"The Ship's Captain Looking over the Rail" is a parable explaining why a man looking at the dawn of a new day should feel that his life's

work has been "to create something dark." The Captain in this parable realizes that he is moved by natural, psychological, even evolutionary forces he does not understand, let alone consciously control
and direct. He knows the truth of the human condition, that "we are
not the captains" of our personal or psychic growth, our fate. This
realization is awesome; but the last line, an exclamatory repetition of
the poem's opening statement, suggests that recognizing man's consciousness as merely the tip of a vast iceberg of obscure but powerful
forces can be both ego-depressing and physically liberating.

"The Dried Sturgeon" is a powerful expression of nature's immense, if unspoken, sense of death and oblivion—much more ancient
and profound than rational man's conscious grieving for his own or
family deaths, or for the mortality even of the entire organic world.
Bly fills the poem with darkness and blackness, and expresses nature's
vastly greater sense of melancholy in this striking, Blakean image:
"The pine tree standing by the roadhouse holds the whole human
night in one needle."

In "A Bouquet of Ten Roses" Bly successfully conveys the reader
from physical to archetypal through language rich in imagery both
sensual and symbolic. The bouquet of ten roses is comprised of nine
(a number symbolic of all physical roses and all the associations their
sensuality suggests) plus one, the dark rose in the bouquet's center,
the thanatos that is the ineluctable shadow side of the rose eros. The
poet moves toward a psychoreligious dimension, invoking the *Gott-
natur*, by conjoining the triumph of the religious art of Chartres with
the divine instinctuality of nature's urge toward procreation in the
final images of "the rose windows of Chartres, the umber moss on the
stag's antlers. . . . " This poem's elegant, involving elaboration upon
the paradoxical rose of love and death is a poetic labor whose conscious craft offers the possibility that through art human consciousness can partially transcend the oblivion of organic nature.

"Visiting Emily Dickinson's Grave with Robert Francis" underscores Bly's linking of his family, the tradition of poets, and the family of man. Strongly reminiscent of Dickinson's ironic "Safe in Their
Alabaster Chambers," this poem too emphasizes the distance and the
difference between man's wishful presumption of immortality and the
incontrovertible reality of mutability and death in nature. Dickinson's
tomb is enclosed by an iron fence decorated with ovals reminding Bly
of "chapel windows on the main Aran island," another notable inter-
section of nature's reality and man's faith. But Bly acknowledges,

quoting Dickinson, that "my family addresses 'an Eclipse every morning, which they call their "Father." ' " And by poem's end "a hump in the ground," an unadorned grave, is the reality man awakens to each morning, not the hoped-for chapel of faith rewarded.

In Bly's poem, as in Dickinson's, the subject of immortality segues into a contemplation of the "immense" psychic distances each person must cross during a lifetime: "The distance is immense, the distances through which Satan and his helpers rose and fell, oh vast areas, the distances between stars, between the first time love is felt in the sleeves of the dress, and the death of the person who was in that room . . . the distance between the feet and head as you lie down, the distance between the mother and father, through which we pass reluctantly." Bly here is not the isolate romantic poet contemplating death, but the man who thinks instinctively of family, who contemplates the nature of life in its human relationships. His conscious incorporation of Dickinson's poetry into his poem not only pays tribute to her continuing life as an artist, but also suggests Bly's respect for the perennial psychoreligious impulse to bridge the immense distance between life and death, an impulse which, as Jung has noted,[5] is so pervasive in human history as to be considered archetypal.

The final poem of part 2, "Finding an Old Ant Mansion," is in some respects a response to the previous poem, for Bly links the creative fecundity of the poet with that of nature itself: both "always thinking" and reshaping material which they have buried within themselves, both driven by natural impulse to "go into dark crevices and live." The poem itself emulates this metamorphic impulse, moving from narration to description, and finally to invention and contemplation.

After admiring the laboring activity of the earth itself, the way it buries everything from a toad to a great man and thus assimilates matter and even time itself into its own life, Bly finds in a pasture a piece of wood, which he carries home and puts on his study desk. At first he perceives the log scientifically, defining it by its measured size and shape; but soon he progresses from observation to metaphor, from science to poetry, no longer studying a two-foot log eaten out by weather and ants, but rather imagining a veritable ant mansion.

As Bly ponders its "sixteen floors," he reworks it, imagining the ant mansion as associated with many aspects of his own life. His language changes from description into a self-conscious tour de force of invention, with the poet exulting in its pure sound—replete with puns, assonance, consonance, and alliteration. This consciously crafted passage serves to highlight the poem's theme of the energetic and unceasing reworking processes of nature—whether performed by rain, ants, or the poetic imagination.

Bly's imaginative rebuilding allows him to declare the ant mansion "a completed soul home," suitable for the ghosts of his own extended family, including ancestors. It will protect them from "the wind of nothing, the wind of Descartes," as well as shelter those suffering from "maternal deprivation," the separation from the anima and her beneficial connection with the ancestral wisdom of the family of man stored in the collective unconscious.[6] Bly declares the ant mansion fit to be his imagined family home, "a place for our destiny." The poetic imagination has destroyed and rebuilt the ant mansion, transforming it into a home through the labor of its creative meditations, in just the same way that the forces of nature are finally seen as, paradoxically, both destructive and creative—"rains and snows, who are themselves ants, who go into dark crevices and live."

Bly here links the poet's creative process with the family, especially the father-son relationship and generationality. The implication of the closing lines is that Bly's poetic labor in a sense redeems his father's work, which is "still unfound" and therefore "open to the rains and snows" for reworking. As Bly's building of language into a poem can redeem the human voice from the oblivion of the unceasing flux, so a consciousness of human generationality can redeem the family from oblivion by remembering/imagining a well-wrought family mansion. The note of redemption is only hinted at here. But the poet's shift of tone toward affirmation becomes immediately evident when this concluding poem is compared to the first poem of part 2, "Eleven O'Clock at Night."

Part 3

Black Coat's two major themes, the family of man and the labor of poets, conjoin to figure prominently in Bly's effort to reconcile fate and free will in part 3. Both themes are imaged in terms of archetypal relationships. The family is not just Bly's mother and father, but the paradigm of mother, father, and son that informs all manifestations of family, from Bly's boyhood in "My Father's Wedding" and "Fifty Males Sitting Together" to God the Father and Christ the Son in "Crazy Carlson's Meadow" and "Kneeling Down to Look Into a Culvert." Similarly, the poet's vocation is described as an archetypal activity, unifying the human community via the magic of language in "Words Rising," and connecting man to the divine Logos ordering the world in "Crazy Carlson's Meadow."

Even more so than in the previous two parts, here Bly is careful to present the anecdotal material about his family history in a larger, psychoreligious context. In "The Grief of Men," for instance, Bly's reference to his father's sister Bertha's dying in childbirth is understood as but one example of grief and death, like many others in history, that are washed by the river of time "past clear / bars and are gone" into the ocean of eternity. And in "Kennedy's Inauguration" Bly's litany of the evils historically caused by intermixing church and state focuses on governmental attacks on the family, the social unit most in competition with the state for people's allegiance. Bly cites the examples of European colonialists in the Congo punishing a black worker by cutting off his son's hands, as well as the Nazis breaking up contraceptive clinics and forcing young women into "breeding hotels" to further Hitler's ambitions for the master race.

But the clearest evidence of Bly's growing intent to see through the material of his family history to the larger pattern of psychic relationships in the archetypal family unit occur in "My Father's Wedding" and "Fifty Males Sitting Together." Bly's dream of his father at the end of "A Meditation on Philosophy" as an "enormous turtle" whose weight is an immobilizing weakness, preventing him from the turning necessary for psychic or evolutionary progress, presents a very different image from that in Bly's essay in *Growing Up,* where the father's weight was equated with strength.[7] The poet-son's dream of his father's weakness, which Bly fears might be his own weakness as well, serves as a prelude to "My Father's Wedding: 1924." This moving poem is an extremely introspective meditation—almost a dream-vision—that quickly progresses through seemingly anecdotal material from Bly's family history (Bly wasn't born until 1926) into the realm of the archetypal. The poem dwells on familiar themes: the nature of father-son relationships and of generationality, as well as the power of fate in limiting man's ability to develop his psyche. Though the poem draws heavily upon the personal for psychic weight and subject, its tone is not intimate, let alone confessional; rather, as in so many of his best poems, Bly's voice has the impersonality of someone who is trying to understand his life in terms of universal patterns.

The speaker's melancholy is evident from the opening line: "lonely for my father." His loneliness arises not simply from the absence of the father, but more so because of the felt lack of something in the speaker's psychic life, a lack caused by his flawed relationship with his father. This poem, like the previous dream, is not simply about Bly's father, but about Bly as his father's son, and about the psychic legacy of father to son through generationality. Bly's father's weakness, his "invisible limp," was his stubborn independence and self-reliance, his doing only what he wanted to do, attitudes generated by what Bly terms ironically his father's "noble loneliness." Bly's father repelled the interdependence, the sympathy, which, in his son's Faulknerian, paradoxical view, "he longed for, didn't need, and wouldn't accept." Bly declares his father's posture of extreme independence to be not strength, but weakness. His father's attitude darkened his marriage and colored his relationship with his son in many unforeseen ways. Because his father hid his psychic limp by pretending an independence so complete no person could have possessed it, somebody else "has to limp it!" Thus Bly exclaims, "Guess where my defect is!"

Bly imagines the marriage of his father and mother, in terms that describe the poet's conception of the psychic configurations that were revealed in that ceremony. Rather than marry a real woman, enter in to the stream of life and thereby submit himself to the risks and possibilities inherent in the struggle to differentiate and integrate the masculine and the feminine within his personality, the father "married the invisible bride." This idealized form of Woman may seem perfection itself; but, since She is static as well as perfect, she effectively denies the bridegroom any chance of growth through the union. Bly compares this idealized, "invisible" bride to an evil woman from a fairy tale, who carried in her breast "the three drops / that wound and kill" the lover. This marriage ceremony is performed by "the man in black," and the words of betrothal are like a "sentence," dooming the bridegroom, bride, and their children to an unhappy psychological relationship. Bly emphasizes this by imagining himself after the wedding holding his father "in my arms for the first time and the last." Physically, of course, Bly has not been born yet; but psychically the son is present at the father's wedding, for it is his father's attitude toward women, nature, and life iself that determines so much of what he will pass on to his son, who will thus have to overcome it in his own personality development.

The father and son "hold" each other after the wedding, for both are committed to each other through generationality from this moment in time forevermore. However, their embrace does not signal a commitment of affection, but of dialectical opposition, for Bly concludes the poem by declaring that after that single moment of union "he was alone / and I was alone." That there were "no friends" attending suggests the ceremony was less a social event than a psychodrama. Certainly, Bly's father's house did not become the conventionally imagined happy home, nor even a place primarily suitable for nurturing and developing feelings. Rather, Bly images it as a "forest, / where both he and I are the hunters."

This poem, in both conception and execution, is one of Bly's best. Through the refiguring of an event fraught with symbolic possibilities, the wedding of his parents, Bly writes a poem that strikes the reader as expressing both the intimate truth of a personal meditation and the public wisdom of a vision of life. The reader feels the profound importance of the relationship between masculine and feminine consciousness, whether in a marriage of two people or the union of two aspects of one personality. The "man in the black coat," who appeared in the book's first poem as an impersonal force of nature, a fate, here seems more closely linked to the free choices possible to human personality, fulfilling the old adage that character is fate. One generation can struggle with and perfect another, just as one man can struggle with and perfect himself. The fact that Bly concludes this poem by acknowledging that he is a "hunter" of his father, for whom he is lonely, suggests that the inexorable march of "the man in the black coat," destiny, the endlessly repeating paradigm described in the folk saying "like father, like son," has been challenged and can be turned by the poet himself.

"Fifty Males Sitting Together" is similar to "My Father's Wedding" in its use of the familial relationship of mother-father-son as a symbol for the corresponding relationship between the feminine and masculine aspects of the individual personality. As day gives way to night at sunset, a man stands on the eastern shore of a lake, looking across at "westward hills" and the "massive / masculine shadow" they now cast, a shadow that seems like an ancient offering to the power of "the resonating night." As the poem develops, the speaker looks inward, reflecting on the relationship between the human family, nature, and the evolution of life itself; just as the woman's "dark" kitchen awaits the drunken husband's return from the world of friends to his family, so too does night overtake the day, and the dark, "blood" wisdom of the collective unconscious permeate and inform the light, rational consciousness in the human psyche. Bly unites these themes, which have all been developed around an imagery of light-dark contrast, when in the final line he looks up from his meditation to discover that "night" has enveloped him.

But Bly extends the light-dark metaphor to the struggle between masculine and feminine conscious within his own psyche. The dark shadow of the first stanza, which had reminded him of "fifty males sitting together," at first appeared to the erstwhile boy-god as a threatening, "coffinlike shadow," Its power menacing his boy-god aloofness. But he contrasts the boisterous, communal activity of the "fifty males sitting together" with the "relaxed, / private" attitude of the lake's isolate reeds and "calm" water. When a reed dies, it "dies alone, as an animal does," not recognizing itself as part of a family that may survive the death of an individual member.

As the reeds protect a calm section of the lake from "motion," so does the protective mother shelter the boy-god from the rhythms of nature and the working community of "fifty males sitting together." He lives as if in another time "thousands of years ago," when mother-consciousness was dominant, before the emergence of masculine consciousness.[8] Thus, he does not know "what the world *wants* from him."

The son-poet is different from the chanting men, and he wonders if he is better or worse for his isolation from the world of masculine consciousness, the rational ego, the "head" which his "blood" realizes "has been cut off." But he asks, has the head been severed from the body, or the body from the head? Neither is meant to dominate the other, but to be united with it.

The poem's conclusion suggests that, finally, he must move to join with the masculine consciousness of the darkness, must struggle to integrate that side of consciousness with the feminine consciousness he has overdeveloped under the tutelage of the protective mother. Just as Bly faulted his father for rejecting his own feminine consciousness, so here he seems to fault himself for living too far from "working men" and masculine consciousness, for being a boy-god aloof from the turbulence of life. The goal of human development, for Bly as for Jung, is the individuation and integration of all aspects of the psyche. Thus, this poem affirms the necessity of a son's learning the wisdom of both father consciousness and mother consciousness, of knowing the complete heritage of the family of man. In this respect it prepares for Bly's turning from Jesus to Odin in the two poems that follow this one to conclude *Black Coat*.

In *Black Coat* Bly balances the power of nature's determinism through heredity over individual behavior, as discussed in the previous two poems, by asserting man's freedom to choose and to affirm himself in such poems as "Words Rising," "Crazy Carlson's Meadow," and "Kneeling Down to Look Into a Culvert." As part 3 moves toward its conclusion, Bly increasingly links the family of man, imagined, with the creative labor of the poet. Bly presents the impulse to make poetry as the natural, human means of asserting the community's and the individual's consciousness against the threatening oblivion of time. In "Words Rising," Bly's most comprehensive statement of the integral relationship of poets and the collective human consciousness, language is the medium uniting the evolutionary family of man, and the various servants of the language are the priests of that evolutionary impulse to affirm consciousness, which is the divine instinctuality of the *Gott-natur* manifesting itself in man.

Dedicated to the poet Richard Eberhart, this poem is a moving statement on the ability of the poet to interfuse the past of the race with his own personal griefs and joys, thereby transforming and even immortalizing his personal life and labor. In stanza 1 Bly images poetic inspiration as a magical "fierceness," the key tone of the book's concluding poems (this image echoes the book's final image conjoining the poet with the "fierce" Christ-Odin figure who dies to redeem mankind); this magical fierceness transforms the poet, allowing him to be in harmony with cosmic forces and human history.

In stanza 2 Bly lyrically expresses the creative alignment of the individual with evolutionary history:

> All those lives we lived in the sunlit
> shelves of the Dordogne, the thousand
> tunes we sang to the skeletons
> of Papua, the many times
> we died—wounded—under the cloak
> of an animal's sniffing, all of these
> return, and the grassy nights
> we ran in the moonlight for hours.

This passage recalls a similar one, with a similar significance, describing the many shelves and crevices of Bly's imagined ancestral home in "Finding an Old Ant Mansion." The archetypal memory of prehistoric experience, including the chthonic wisdom of the "old earth fragrance," comes "welling up" through the most elemental words of language itself.

In stanza 4 Bly borrows a famous image from Plato's *Ion* for the poet: a bee, making the honey of "language" for the tribal hive out of his personal joys and griefs, emotions that in the evolutionary process had to be learned by all men "before we could invent the wheel." Language is the honey wherein lies stored the archetypal memories, and the poet is the man who, inspired by this greater force, can reclaim them by transforming his individual life into language until "words grow" and symbolize for the reader the collective wisdom.

The poem concludes with a stanza of praise for the poetic spirit in all its manifestations:

> Blessings then on the man who labors
> in his tiny room, writing stanzas on the lamb;
> blessings on the woman, who picks the brown
> seeds of solitude in afternoon light
> out of the black seeds of loneliness.
> And blessings on the dictionary maker, huddled among
> his bearded words, and on the setter of songs
> who sleeps at night inside his violin case.

Blessed are the man or woman who performs the creative, transforming act, the poets "writing stanzas on the lamb," honoring Christ's redemptive sacrifice by themselves sacrificing their personal emotions to expression of the collective wisdom. And blessed too, says Bly, are the "dictionary maker" and the "setter of songs." Bly images this latter as both the instrument of music and the music itself, thus invoking a long tradition of poetic conceits for the relationship of poet and poem. Bly here compares the successful artist to the successful person—both creating a unity out of a diversity of materials; and his pronouncement of "Blessings" on them suggests that both activities confer on the psyche a kind of spiritual harmony, a state of grace.

Certainly, Bly's most compelling assertion of the psychoreligious nature of the poet's calling to redeem human consciousness, and thereby the family of man, from nature's law of inevitable death occurs in the concluding two poems of *Black Coat*. There, Bly presents the relationship between God the Father and His Son as symbolic of the family relationship through generationality. Further, he associates the divine instinctuality of nature, identified elsewhere as the *Gott-nature*, with the Logos, the divine word which is the ordering principle both of nature and, through language and poetry, of the family of man, imagined. Bly images the redeemer-poet as a fierce, phoenixlike creature destined to be destroyed and reborn over and over in his struggle to raise to light the dark, unconscious wisdom of his psyche and of the human race.

In the penultimate poem of the book, "Crazy Carlson's Meadow," Bly presents the macrocosmic aspect of his poetic theme of the son's search for reconciliation and union with the father. Bly carefully images the struggle for unified consciousness in both mythic and conventionally religious terms. The poem limns the failure of classical mythology or the Christian religion to explain the world satisfactorily to modern man, to find a place in the "too pure and blue" sky that modern man has projected upon the heavens. This empty blue sky, as much a metaphor for contemporary consciousness as Stevens's "mind of winter" which Bly had invoked in earlier poems, is inhabited by a lonely young man "alone," without either the moon or the resonating night's darkness, let alone their attendant wisdom. Crazy Carlson is a Bly invention who carries associations with Christ, perhaps Bly's father, and even Yeats's "Crazy Jane"; but his main identity is as someone who cut down the trees "back to the dark firs" to make a meadow, who cleared some psychic territory for mankind. By skillfully building associations around the contrast of blue sky and dark firs, Bly shows Christ as having taught men the importance of clearing a space for feminine consciousness in human culture and human personality. However, for Bly Christ failed to get beyond the preliminary stage of championing the values of feminine consciousness for the psyche. Christ failed to reach his "father's house," to convince a masculine-dominant Western culture of the truth of a deeper wisdom, imaged here as "words hidden" within the darkness of death itself. Christ's psychic "journey toward the Father" by the path of honoring feminine consciousness was opposed by two masculine-dominant cultures, by the Jews who "refused" to acknowledge Jesus's divine "energies" and by the Romans, whose Crucifixion of Christ made him quiver "like an aspen leaf before the storm of Empire." Christ's failure soured "the wine of Cana," symbolic of the marriage sacrament uniting masculine and feminine consciousness in the family. Christ's message of twofold consciousness did not take hold in Western culture; its failure to be transmitted is imaged as Christ's failure to become the father, whose seed begets the future. Bly wishes "Blessings on you, my king," but he declares also that "all consequences" of Christ's death are now "finished," with "the lake closed / again, as before the leaf fell, all forgiven, the path ended." The motionless lake, the fallen aspen leaf, and the path all have resonances within the poetry of this book.

The poem's conclusion returns to the contemporary human condition, where "each young man" has to struggle "alone" against a similar configuration of forces; but now they are ignorant of "the absent / moon," the White Goddess of feminine consciousness worshipped in ancient times. Further, they lack the "learning" acquired on a cross by another image of divinity, that "fierce male" Norse god Odin, who created the cosmos and rules over wisdom, war, art, culture, and the dead. Bly here envisions the significance of Odin's sacrificial death on the World Ash tree Yggdrasil as similar to that elucidated by his friend and mentor the Jungian comparative mythologist Joseph Campbell,[9] who links the Norse myth with "the Buddha beneath the Tree of Enlightenment (the Bo Tree) and Christ on Holy Rood (the Tree of Redemption)" as "analogous figures, incorporating an archetypal World Savior, World Tree motif [of] immemorial antiquity."[10] Odin serves Bly's symbolic purposes well, for he combines the functions divided between father and son in Christianity; Odin the "all-father" is not only god the father but also the divine sacrifice made to god the father. As the *Havamal* lay in the Norse/Icelandic poems of the *Elder Edda* describes it, Odin is "given to Odin, / myself to myself." This sacrifice is a mysterious initiation ritual of at-onement of self, divinity, and death in which Odin is "reborn fortified with the knowledge which belongs to the dead."[11] The symbol of Odin's achievement of death and rebirth are the "runes," magical words preserved through writing that were intended primarily to work spells, and which made Odin or the poet-shaman of his cult powerful enough to make dead men talk. Odin endured his death struggle in order to see through the darkness to what Bly calls here the "words hidden" within "the folds of darkness," the essential truth governing and uniting all aspects of the universe, whether it be named Christ's "Father," St. John's "Logos," Odin's "runes," or Whitman's "innermost word, death." Bly's epithet "fierce" will link the redemptive art of this "fierce male" god with the poet himself in the next poem, as it links him to the "fierceness" with which Bly had identified poetic inspiration in "Words Rising."

The final poem of the book, "Kneeling Down to Look into a Culvert," presents a resonating conclusion to many of the book's images and themes. The lake symbolic of the unconscious, from which the poet emerges as a metamorphosing "water-serpent"; the imagery of light and shadow; the relationship between fathers and sons; the fierceness of the poetic process leading through death to resurrection (and recalling faintly the image of "a fierce man on his deathbed," which closed the opening poem of Bly's very first book, *Silence*)—all work in *Black Coat's* concluding poem with an incremental strength gained from their earlier appearances.

"Kneeling Down to Look into a Culvert" stands as an important statement of Bly's view of the correspondences between the microcosmic processes of the poetic imagination and the macrocosmic processes of life itself, between fathering new poems and fathering children to continue the family of man. The poet, looking into a culvert half-filled with water, sees a "cone of light," and this begets the poem's first, striking conceit:

> I kneel down to peer into a culvert.
> The other end seems far away.
> One cone of light floats in the shadowed water.
> This is how our children will look when we are dead.

He wonders if he is finished begetting children. He walks farther, into a plowed field holding "a lake newly made." He says he has seen this same lake before, that he returns to it "each time my children are grown." This cyclical process of fathering and raising a child, watching him leave home, then returning to the original lake to father another one, leads the poet-hero to compare himself to a "water-serpent," a dragon creature who lives in the lake and who lives through many emergences and metamorphoses. Jung has noted that in certain mythologies, including the Norse, where "the hero is recognized by the fact that he has snake's eyes, . . . the hero is himself the dragon,"[12] which emphasizes that his struggle is between two parts of one whole. Similarly, Bly's poem depicts the poet-hero as living in the "arctic" lake of his unconsciousness, "alone" for "a thousand years"; but eventually, and always, over and over, "a feathery head pokes from the water." Reenacting a millennial battle, the poet responds to the challenge of the new creature emerging from his lake; he fights him, declaring "it's time—it's right," and is "torn to pieces fighting."

In this comparison the lake is the poet's collective unconscious, from which spring the eternal archetypal patterns. The children are not merely physical offspring, but his poems as well—both products of a fierce, dialectical struggle. The fight at the poem's end is the ritual reenactment of the archetypal sacrificial fight that leads through death to rebirth: it finds its parallels in the Odin-Dionysus-Christ figure of "Crazy Carlson's Meadow." Here Bly skillfully blends two themes: the father-son relationship, with its overtones of inevitable struggle and death, and the poetic process as the paradigm for the psyche's living by the perpetual synthesis of, and therefore transcendence of, opposites.[13] This possibility of man's turning, defying life's deterministic forces, which was only hinted at in the book's beginning, has come more and more to be symbolized not only by the natural, evolutionary change inherent in generationality, but also by the artist's act of assimilating and evolving beyond his experience by embodying it in a consciously created artifact, a poem. Indeed, the etymology of "verse" identifies it as a form of turning. Thus, "Kneeling Down to Look into a Culvert" finds an effective symbol for this death-resurrection motif in the final image of the millennial, ever-renewing battle.

The conclusion of *Black Coat,* not only in its theme of the poet as hero but also in its tone of finality, is a declaration about Bly's career to date as well as about this book. The poet's resolution might be described best by a phrase used to explain the pagan attitude of the Norse god Thor, the last god left alive on the Norse Doomsday, as he faces a cosmic battle that he knows he is doomed to lose. Thor "will fight against the serpent who surrounds the world. He will strike the beast and step back dying, but not dismayed."[14] The lay describing this battle declares that after the destruction of the gods, the world will rise again from the sea, renewed; however, the forces of evil that brought on the Doomsday will also survive, so that the event can happen over and over again. The tone of Bly's poem invokes a similar sense of destruction and rebirth, and the poet-hero's acceptance of death but not defeat may be based on an awareness of the cyclical nature of the pattern in time, as well as the psychical nature of the battle itself: in a sense, as Jung noted, the hero's enemy is a part of himself. This tone of finality accompanies the reconciliation of Bly's two opposing themes in this poem, so that the poet's final, fierce affirmation, "I fight—it's time—it's right," is aptly countered by "and am torn to pieces fighting." The poem's placement at the end of the book, as well as its style and subject, give it an incremental authenticity and strength that confirms the reader's sense of being in the presence of major poetry. The conflicts inherent in the poem's dominant themes have been reconciled, at least momentarily, under the aegis of the artist's claim for his work as a justification of his life. Bly has found, and now affirms, a new use for his poetry. For Bly poetry is not separate from and greater than ordinary life, not a way to escape nature's destiny; rather, it is a human way to enter into the stream of nature's energies. He emphasizes the correspondence between the process of poetic creation and two similar, natural processes. In *Black Coat* the more immediate process is that of sons acknowledging, assimilating, and going beyond fathers in the evolving generations of the family of man. But implicit in this, and fundamental to it, is the exploration of the geography of the psyche necessary for its journey toward integration. Bly's lifelong journey on the inward road is not only the perduring theme of his career, but also the basis of his poetic and personal achievement.

Chapter Seven
Redefining the American Poet

In his seventh decade, Robert Bly has shown no signs of diminishing creativity or unwillingness to journey in new directions. His *Selected Poems* marked a plateau, but not a conclusion, to his forty-year career as a man of letters. Not only new accomplishments, but also further recognitions and awards, undoubtedly await him. Whatever the future holds, any assessment of the achievement of Robert Bly to date must focus on three major areas.

A career is the work of a lifetime, and Robert Bly is one of the few Americans whose life's work justifies the title of poet. His career exemplifies the best of his generation, not only for its long fidelity to his vocation, but also for its example to, and influence upon, others. In a sense, Bly's career redefined the role of the poet for his generation, providing a comprehensive definition of what that vocation might involve. To cite just a few instances in which Bly's example became the model, one might mention the poet's founding of his own magazine and publishing house, or his turning to political poetry and public demonstration during the social crisis of the Vietnam War, or his thirty-year-long labor of translating and promulgating the work of foreign poets to insular Americans, or his development and popularization of the prose poem, or even his choice of a life-style, living on a remote farm and refusing to work for or submit to the university.

However important Bly's career as a man of letters, including his influence upon others, seems today, it will ultimately prove secondary to his achievement as an American poet. As he once wrote of his father, Bly carried the burden a little bit higher up the mountain; he took classic American themes and reinterpreted them for his time. Bly is squarely within the American romantic tradition of Emerson, Whitman, and Hart Crane in his belief that the poet's lifelong task is the elucidation of the human soul. Further, Bly emulates Thoreau in his belief in the integral relationship between the individual psyche and the body politic, and in his concomitant willingness to engage at the psychospiritual level the political issues of his time. Bly not only knows and follows these American poetic traditions, he also writes about them. In his later work, especially, he takes pains to locate himself within a poetic tradition. He has come to write more and more of this centrality of the family of poets to the continuity of the family of man. In this Bly seeks to renew and reaffirm in his poetry the importance of the traditional interdependence of life and the language arts.

Finally, and most importantly, Robert Bly's achievement must rest upon what new elements his vision and his poetic voice have added to the commonweal. It is good, but not sufficient for poetic immortality, to influence one's contemporaries or reaffirm the tradition. Robert Bly's originality lies in his lifelong journey through his psyche toward the goal of personality development, toward selfhood; his achievement lies in his exploration and re-creation in poetry of an imaginative geography of the human psychic landscape. Bly's inward road has taken him along the process that Jung described as individuation and integration; Bly has been faithfully attentive to the unfolding of the many aspects of his developing personality, as well as to his continuing struggle to integrate them into a complete yet multiplicitous soul. To the enduring poetic subjects of nature, politics, the soul, God, the family, death, and human love Robert Bly has brought a constant source of light: himself. Further, he has consciously sought out more universal symbols for the expression of his own psychic journey, since he believes with Jung that the individual and subjective life is always amplified and illuminated when shown against the backdrop of the universal and archetypal. The ultimate achievement of Robert Bly is that at its best his poetry succeeds in awakening, even inspiring, his audience with a sense of human community and possibility that is both psychological and, in the most fundamental sense, religious. Let this stand as his achievement, that sometimes within the spell of his poetry the ancient, elusive dream of aligning perfectly the conscious and unconscious parts of human nature seems almost true: "For we are like the branch bent in the water . . . / Taken out, it is whole, it was always whole. . . ."

Notes and References

Chapter One

1. Charles Altieri, *Self and Sensibility in Contemporary American Poetry* (Cambridge: Cambridge University Press, 1984), 8.
2. Charles Molesworth, *The Fierce Embrace* (Columbia, Mo., 1979), 113.
3. William Matthews, "Thinking about Robert Bly," *Tennessee Poetry Journal* 2, no. 2 (Winter 1969), 49.
4. Ibid.
5. Ibid.
6. In *Growing Up in Minnesota: Ten Writers Remember Their Childhoods,* ed. Chester G. Anderson (Minneapolis: University of Minnesota Press, 1976), 211; hereafter cited in the text as *Growing.*
7. For another Bly's Minnesota, see Carol Bly, *Letters From the Country* (New York: Harper & Row, 1981), 1–184, passim.
8. Deborah Baker, "Making a Farm: A Literary Biography," in *Of Solitude and Silence: Writings on Robert Bly,* ed. Richard Jones and Kate Daniels (Boston, 1981), 36.
9. Bob Ehlert, "Robert Bly," *Minneapolis Star and Tribune,* Sunday Magazine, 20 January, 1985, 10.
10. James Hillman, who has influenced Bly, develops Jung's idea of soul and soul-making as the crucial, evolving relationship between one's consciousness and his self, which combines both conscious and unconscious, in *Re-Visioning Psychology* (New York: Harper & Row, 1975), 165–229, passim.
11. This important image occurs in *Sleepers Joining Hands* (New York, 1973), 59; hereafter cited in the text as *S.*
12. "In Search of an American Muse," *New York Times Book Review,* 22 January, 1984, 1, 29.
13. Louis Simpson, *North of Jamaica* (New York: Harper & Row, 1972), 241–42.
14. Cf. "The Man Whom the Sea Kept Awake," *Paris Review,* Spring–Summer 1957, 141, and "The Possibility of New Poetry," ibid., April 1960, 31.
15. See *Talking All Morning* (Ann Arbor, 1980), 14–15, hereafter, cited in the text as *T.*
16. C. G. Jung, in *Memories, Dreams, Reflections,* trans. Richard and Clara Winston, ed. Aniela Jaffe (New York: Vantage Books, 1963), viii–ix, explains this title.
17. Molesworth, *The Fierce Embrace,* 113.

18. "Interview With the Head of *The New York Times Book Review*," *Fifties* 1 (1958):47.

19. "Award," *Fifties* 2 (1959):51.

20. "Award," *Fifties* 3 (1959):57.

21. "Wax Museum," *Sixties* 4 (1960):30–31.

22. "Wax Museum," *Fifties* 1 (1958):40.

23. "Wax Museum," *Fifties* 3 (1959):52.

24. "Award," *Sixties* 5 (1961):91.

25. "On the Necessary Aestheticism of Modern Poetry," *Sixties* 6 (1962):23.

26. "Five Decades of Modern American Poetry," Fifties 1 (1958), 38.

27. Robert Kelly, "Interview," in *The Sullen Art,* ed. David Ossman (New York: Corinth Books, 1963), 34.

28. George S. Lensing and Ronald Moran, *Four Poets of the Emotive Imagination* (Baton Rouge, 1976), 40.

29. Lensing and Moran, *Four Poets,* 59.

30. Crunk, "The Work of Donald Hall," *Fifties* 3 (1959):32–46; hereafter, cited in the text.

31. Crunk, "The Work of James Dickey," *Sixties* 7 (1964):41–57; hereafter cited in the text.

32. "The Collapse of James Dickey," *Sixties* 9 (1967):70–79; hereafter cited in the text.

33. Robert Pinsky, *The Situation of Poetry* (Princeton: Princeton University Press, 1976), 78.

Chapter Two

1. Bly, James Wright, and William Duffy, *The Lion's Tail and Eyes: Poems Written Out of Laziness and Silence* (Madison, Minnesota: Sixties Press, 1962), 35–45.

2. *Silence in the Snowy Fields* (Middletown, Conn., 1962); hereafter cited in the text as *Si.*

3. John Logan, "Poetry Shelf," *Critic* 21 (January 1963):84.

4. *The Lion's Tail and Eyes,* note on dust jacket.

5. Ibid., 6.

6. Ibid.

7. The British edition of *Silence* has significant changes, including five, rather than three, sections. Eighteen pages have been added, and Bly has reshaped the book by changing the order of the poems.

8. "Five Decades of Modern American Poetry," 38. This is Bly's term for the poetry that others refer to as surrealism, "deep image" poetry, or poetry of "the emotive imagination" or "radical presence."

9. "In Search of an American Muse," 1, 29.

10. Hillman, *Re-Visioning Psychology,* ix; also, my 145, n. 10.

11. Erich Neumann, *The Great Mother: An Analysis of the Archetype,* trans. Ralph Manheim (New York: Bollingen Foundation, 1963), xliii.

12. Pinsky, *The Situation of Poetry,* 77.

13. "The Surprise of Neruda," *Sixties* (1964), 7:18.

14. "The Dead World and the Live World," *Sixties* 8 (1966):6.

15. Ibid., 5.

16. Robert Kelly, "Notes on the Poetry of Deep Image," *Trobar: a magazine of the new poetry* 2 (1961):14.

17. Kelly, "Interview," 35.

18. "Interview," in *Sullen Art,* ed. Ossman, 41.

19. Jerome Rothenberg, "Interview," in ibid., 30–31.

20. Ossman, in ibid., 30, n.

21. Lensing and Moran, *Four Poets,* 1–70 passim.

22. Ibid., 9.

23. "A Wrong Turning in American Poetry," *Choice* 3 (1963):40.

24. Altieri, *Enlarging the Temple* (Lewisburg, Pa., 1979),78; immediately following page references in the text.

25. Jung, *Memories, Dreams, Reflections,* 196.

26. Letter to Friberg, in *Moving Inward* (Göteborg, Sweden, 1977), 5n. Bly has given various dates for his initial interest in Jung. He once claimed that the seemingly Jungian "A Man Writes to a Part of Himself," published in 1962 in *Silence,* was written "before he started reading Jung" (cited in James Mersmann, *Out of the Vietnam Vortex* [Lawrence, 1979], 133 n.).

27. Mersmann, *Out of the Vietnam Vortex,* 133.

28. *Memories, Dreams, Reflections,* 186.

29. "The Attack on the Old Position," in *News of the Universe: Poems of Twofold Consciousness* (San Francisco, 1980), 35; hereafter cited in the text as *N.*

30. "Leaving the House," in ibid., 251.

Chapter Three

1. *The Light around the Body* (New York, 1967); hereafter cited in the text as *L.*

2. For a leftist's assessment of Bly as "wrong in thinking that the inner regions are outside politics," see Todd Gitlin, "The Return of Political Poetry," *Commonweal* 94 (23 July 1971):376.

3. *Forty Poems Touching on Recent American History* (Madison, Minn., 1966), 7–17; hereafter cited in the text as *F.*

4. *A Poetry Reading Against the Vietnam War* (Madison, Minn., 1966); hereafter cited in the text as *P.*

5. See "On Pablo Neruda," *Nation* 206 (25 March 1968):4 14–18.

6. This thesis is elaborated on by Louis Z. Hammer, "Moths in the Light," *Kayak,* April, 1968, 67.

7. See "The Collapse of James Dickey."

8. Donald Hall, Harvey Shapiro, and Theodore Weiss cited in "The National Book Awards," *Nation* 206 (25 March 1968):414.

9. Robert S. McNamara, "Memo of May 19, 1967 to President Lyndon Johnson," cited in "Libel Trial Offers Vietnam Revelations," by Joe Starita, *Miami Herald,* 25 December 1984, 11.

10. Altieri, *Self and Sensibility,* 4.

11. "The Work of James Dickey," 50.

12. Howard Nelson, *Robert Bly* (New York, 1984),49–52.

13. Letter to the author, 19 December 1984.

14. C. G. Jung, *Collected Works,* 2d ed., trans. R. F. C. Hull, ed. Sir Herbert Read, Michael Fordham, and Gerhard Adler (Princeton: Princeton University Press, 1966), 7:188. Hereafter, all references will be to *Collected Works* by volume number and page.

15. "The Three Brains," in *Leaping Poetry* (Boston, 1975), 59–67.

16. Jung, *Collected Works,* 7:114.

17. Jung defines the shadow as "the 'negative' side of the personality, the sum of all those unpleasant qualities we like to hide, together with the insufficiently developed functions and the contents of the personal unconscious" (*Collected Works,* 7:66, n.).

18. Adele Bloch, "Virgil's Heroes: Descent into Madness," *Journal of Evolutionary Psychology* 5, nos. 3–4 (August 1984):153.

19. Gitlin, "The Return of Political Poetry," 377.

20. Mersmann suggests Freud's essay "Thoughts on War and Death" as a possible source for Bly's analysis (*Out of the Vietnam Vortex,* 262, n. 21.).

21. "The Satisfaction of Vietnam: A Play in Eight Scenes," *Chelsea* 24–25 (October 1968):43.

22. Gitlin, "The Return of Political Poetry," 377.

23. Bly describes the poem's genesis and the significance of "instants" in *Talking,* 88.

Chapter Four

1. *The Teeth-Mother Naked at Last* (San Francisco: City Lights Books, 1970); references are to the later version contained in *Sleepers,* 18–26.

2. Nelson, *Robert Bly,* 51.

3. Joyce Carol Oates, "Where They All Are Sleeping," *Modern Poetry Studies* 4 (1973):341.

4. Molesworth, *The Fierce Embrace,* 126.

5. Nelson, *Robert Bly,* 87.

6. Bly's dramatic techniques, as well as many of the poem's words and

images, appeared earlier in his play "The Satisfaction of Vietnam." Compare the symbolism of the "Bachofen bomb" (37) with *Sleepers*, 29.

7. See also "The Three Brains," in *Leaping Poetry*, 59–67. For an analysis of the "three brain" theory, see William V. Davis, " 'At the Edges of the Light,' " in *Of Solitude and Silence*, ed. Jones and Daniels, 257–59, 264–65, nn. 11–13.

8. C. G. Jung, preface to *Psyche and Symbol*, ed. Violet Laszlo (New York: Doubleday Anchor Books, 1958), 8.

9. Jung, *Collected Works*, 6:94, discusses this projection phenomenon; see also 204 for his analysis of "mass-suggestions against which the individual is helpless."

10. Baker, "Making a Farm," 66.

11. For a thorough presentation of this "monomyth" and its psychospiritual implications, one that illuminates Bly's poem at many points, see Joseph Campbell, *The Hero With a Thousand Faces*, 2d ed. (Princeton: Princeton University Press, 1968), 49–245 passim. See also Michael Atkinson, "Robert Bly's *Sleepers Joining Hands*: Shadow and Self," *Iowa Review* 7 (Fall 1976):135–53, for a close account of the poem's use of Jung.

12. See Atkinson, "Shadow and Self," 145.

13. Nelson, *Robert Bly*, 99.

14. Along with Atkinson, these include David Seal, "Waking to 'Sleepers Joining Hands,' " in *Of Solitude and Silence*, ed. Jones and Daniels, 219–48, which analyzes how "Sleepers" both adheres to and varies from the Jung-Campbell model.

15. Jung, *Collected Works*, 6:192.

16. Ibid., 6:304.

17. Ibid., 6:192.

18. Ibid., 9:284n.

19. Ibid., 6:53–54.

20. Ibid., 6:177.

21. Cf. Campbell, *Hero With a Thousand Faces*, 95.

22. Cf. ibid., 91.

23. Cf. ibid., 73.

24. Cf. ibid., 90–95, esp. fig. 5.

Chapter Five

1. *The Morning Glory* (New York, 1975) incorporates *The Morning Glory: Another Thing That Will Never Be My Friend* (San Francisco: Kayak Press, 1969–70) and *Point Reyes Poems* (Half Moon Bay, Calif.: Mudra Press, 1974).

2. William V. Davis, " 'In a Low Voice' " *Midwest Quarterly* 25, no. 2 (1984):149–52, discusses the history and poetic validity of the prose poem form.

3. "Recognizing the Image as a Form of Intelligence" *Field* 24 (Spring 1981):18.

4. *This Body is Made of Camphor and Gopherwood* (New York, 1979).

5. Molesworth, *The Fierce Embrace,* 130.

6. See Philip Dacey, "This Book Is Made of Turkey Soup and Star Music," *Parnassus,* Fall–Winter 1978, 34–45.

7. *Old Man Rubbing His Eyes* is reprinted in *This Tree Will Be Here for a Thousand Years* (New York, 1979); hereafter cited in the text as *Tr.*

8. "Recognizing the Image," 18.

9. Ibid., 21.

10. Bly's "Being a Lutheran Boy-god in Minnesota" is an informing presence behind the family poems of this period, especially in its description of Bly's socioreligious role in a Lutheran, Norwegian-American culture that repressed all doctrinal conflict with what Bly found to be a "maddening cheerfulness" (*Growing Up in Minnesota,* ed. Anderson, 211).

11. Bly has translated the work of more than twenty poets, and has written an excellent book on the process and its challenges: *The Eight Stages of Translation* (Boston, 1983).

Chapter Six

1. *The Man in the Black Coat Turns* (New York, 1981).

2. In *Growing Up in Minnesota,* ed. Anderson, pp. 205–19. Hereafter cited in the text as *G.*

3. "In Search of an American Muse," 29.

4. "Out of the Rolling Ocean," in *Loving a Woman in Two Worlds* (New York, 1985), 1.

5. Jung, *Collected Works,* 7:191–92.

6. Jung describes the anima, man's connection with the collective unconscious, as "all life that has been in the past and is still alive in him" (*Memories, Dreams, Reflections,* 286).

7. Bly offers a mixed compliment, praising his father for abjuring "easy judgments. . . . He preferred weight, even if the stone sank all the way to the bottom" (*G,* 206).

8. Bly argues this development from matriarchies to patriarchies as historical fact in *Sleepers,* 29.

9. Bly has acknowledged that "as a student of myth, I'm a child of Joseph Campbell's " (*Robert Bly,* ed. Peseroff, 316).

10. Campbell, *Hero with a Thousand Faces,* 33, n. 37. See also 191, n. 169; 235, n. 31; and 259–60, esp. n. 7.

11. E. O. G. Turville-Petre, *Origins of Icelandic Literature* (Oxford: Clarendon Press, 1953), 17. For a more likely source see Campbell, *Hero with a Thousand Faces,* 259–60, esp. n. 7.

12. C. G. Jung, *Analytical Psychology: Its Theory and Practice* (New York: Pantheon Books, 1968), 102–3.

13. Late in life Jung declared man's psychic life to be one of "the struggle and reconciliation of opposites," for it is "set up in accord with the structure of the universe," and thus follows the macrocosm's model of "the universal conflict of opposites" (*Memories, Dreams, Reflections,* 335).

14. Turville-Petre, *Origins of Icelandic Literature,* 58.

Selected Bibliography

PRIMARY SOURCES

1. Poetry

Jumping Out of Bed. Barre, Mass.: Barre Publishers, 1973.

The Light around the Body. New York: Harper & Row, 1967. London: Rapp & Whiting, 1968.

Loving a Woman in Two Worlds. New York: Dial Press, 1985.

The Man in the Black Coat Turns. New York: Dial Press, 1981.

The Morning Glory. New York: Harper & Row, 1975.

Selected Poems. New York: Harper & Row, 1986.

Silence in the Snowy Fields. Middletown, Conn.: Wesleyan University Press, 1962; London: Cape, 1967.

Sleepers Joining Hands. New York: Harper & Row, 1973.

This Body Is Made of Camphor and Gopherwood. New York: Harper & Row, 1979.

This Tree Will Be Here for a Thousand Years. New York: Harper & Row, 1979.

2. Other Books

The Eight Stages of Translation. Boston: Rowan Tree Press, 1983. Applies to Bly's own recent poetry as well as to his translations.

Forty Poems Touching on Recent American History. Edited by Robert Bly. Madison, Minn.: Sixties Press, 1966. Contains "Leaping Up into Political Poetry," 7–17.

Leaping Poetry: An Idea with Poems and Translations. Boston: Beacon Press, 1975. Useful essays on poetics.

News of the Universe: Poems of Twofold Consciousness. San Francisco: Sierra Club Books, 1980. A readable, teachable anthology with helpful essays introducing Bly's version of literary psychohistory since 1700.

A Poetry Reading against the Vietnam War. Edited with David Ray. Madison, Minn.: American Writers against the Vietnam War/Sixties Press, 1966.

Talking All Morning. Ann Arbor: University of Michigan Press, 1980. An indispensable presentation of Bly talking through essays and interviews.

3. Translations

Basho: Twelve Poems. San Francisco: Mudra Press, 1972.

Friends, You Drank Some Darkness: Martinson, Ekelof, and Transtromer. Boston: Beacon Press, 1975.

The Kabir Book: 44 of the Ecstatic Poems of Kabir. Boston: Beacon Press, 1977.
Lorca and Jiminez: Selected Poems. Boston: Beacon Press, 1973.
Mirabai: Six Versions. New York: Red Ozier Press, 1980.
Neruda and Vallejo: Selected Poems. Boston: Beacon Press, 1971. With James
   Wright and John Knoepfle.
Selected Poems of Antonio Machado. Middletown, Conn.: Wesleyan University
   Press, 1985.
Selected Poems of Rainer Maria Rilke. New York: Harper & Row, 1981.
Twenty Poems of Georg Trakl. Madison, Minn.: Sixties Press, 1961. With
   James Wright.
Twenty Poems of Rolf Jacobsen. Madison, Minn.: Sixties Press, 1977.

SECONDARY SOURCES

1. Bibliographies
Doss, James, and Daniels, Kate. "Selected Bibliography." In *Of Solitude
   and Silence,* edited by R. Jones and K. Daniels; 268–76. Boston: Beacon
   Press, 1981. The best bibliography.

2. Books, Parts of Books, and Articles
Altieri, Charles. *Enlarging the Temple.* Lewisburg, Pa.: Bucknell University
   Press, 1979. Immanence in Bly and others.
Atkinson, Michael. "*Sleepers Joining Hands:* Shadow and Self." *Iowa Review*
   7, no. 4 (Fall 1976):135–53. A balanced Jungian analysis.
Baker, Deborah. "Making a Farm: A Literary Biography." In *Of Solitude
   and Silence,* edited by R. Jones and K. Daniels, 33–78. Boston: Beacon
   Press, 1981. An interesting survey of Bly's life.
Friberg, Ingegard. *Moving Inward: A Study of Robert Bly's Poetry.* Göteborg,
   Sweden: Acta Universitatis Gothoburgensis, 1977. Comprehensive im-
   age analysis, long bibliography.
Jones, Richard and Daniels, Kate, ed. *Of Solitude and Silence: Writings on
   Robert Bly.* Boston: Beacon Press, 1981. A good miscellany, with help-
   ful articles by Baker, Davis, and Seal, and the most complete bibliog-
   raphy.
Lensing, George S., and Moran, Ronald. *Four Poets of the Emotive Imagina-
   tion: Robert Bly, James Wright, Louis Simpson, and William Stafford.* Baton
   Rouge: Louisiana State University Press, 1976. Bly's early poetics.
Mersmann, James F. *Out of the Vietnam Vortex.* Lawrence: University of
   Kansas Press, 1974. A chapter on Bly and Vietnam.
Molesworth, Charles. *The Fierce Embrace: A Study of Contemporary American
   Poetry.* Columbia: University of Missouri Press, 1979. A well-written
   argument for Bly's spiritual impulse.

"National Book Awards." *Nation* 206 (25 March 1968):413–14. An account of Bly's most memorable (and illegal) political protest.

Nelson, Howard. *Robert Bly: An Introduction to the Poetry.* New York: Columbia University Press, 1984. An appreciative introduction.

Ohio Review 19, no. 3 (Fall 1978):29–66. Feature on Bly.

Peseroff, Joyce, ed. *Robert Bly: When Sleepers Awake.* Ann Arbor: University of Michigan Press, 1984. A generous collection of interviews and essays, several previously unpublished.

Rexroth, Kenneth. "The Poet as Responsible." *Northwest Review* 9 (Fall–Winter 1967–68):116–18. Justifies Bly's political poetry.

San Francisco Book Review, no 19 (April 1971): 1–32.

Tennessee Poetry Journal 2, no. 2 (Winter 1969). Robert Bly issue. A good image of Bly as a literary phenomenon, circa 1969.

Index

Aeneas, 56
Altieri, Charles, 1, *27–28,* 42
American Writers Against the Vietnam War, 2, 14, 16, 41, 46
Andromeda, 89
anima, archetype of, 33, 52, 65–66, 82, *85,* 130, 150n6
Apollo, 80
archetype, *85, 89,* 135–36, 140
Ark, 109
Artemis, 82
Ashbery, John, 5
Auden, W. H., 13, 123, 126
"Award of the Blue Toad, The," 9–10

Bachofen, J. J., 31, 79, 82
Baker, Debra, 4
Basho, 121, 128
Baudelaire, Charles, 126
Beacon Press, 38
Beatrice, 82
Beowulf, 79, 100
Benn, Gottfried, 11
Big Table, 8
Black Mountain Review, 8
Blake, William, 121, 128
Bly, Robert, archetypal past, theme of, 18–19, 22, 32, 64, 73, 76–78, *84–87,* 91, 100, 101, 110, 123–24, 135–36, 140; image, *26–31,* 87, 146n8; imagery, animal, 45–46; imagery, psychohistorical, *44–46,* 59, 88; imagery, psychoreligious, 59, 61, *62–63,* 87, 108–9, *111–12,* 118–19, 120, 123, 126, 128, 129, 131, 136–41; imagery, religious: apocalypse, 68–69, atonement, 60–61, 138, *felix culpa,* 62, God, 98–99, 100, 101, 102, 104, 109, *111–12,* 143, baptism, 99, theodicy, 102–3,

Passover, 98, Prodigal Son, 126, grace, 136–37, Odin-Christ, 138–40, Crucifixion, 133–38; "inward road," theme of, 3, 4, 5, 18–19, 32, 51, 58, 61, 67, 77–78, 100, 110, 111–12, 141; literary criticism, 2, *9–17,* 38–40, 150n3; politics and poetry, *11–17,* 39–42, 46–47; reputation, 1–2, 142–43; "snowy fields" symbol, 26, *29,* 48, 60, 115–16; symbolic origins: *Fifties, 8–17,* 37, 38, 46, Harvard/New York, *5–7,* 95, Minnesota, *3–5,* 21, 32, 37, 118, 124–25, Norway, *7–8,* 32, 138, "wound," childhood, 4, 132

WORKS—POETRY:
"After Drinking All Night With a Friend, We Go Out in a Boat at Dawn To See Who Can Write the Best Poem," 22, 25
"After the Industrial Revolution, All Things Happen At Once," 49–50
"After Working," 6, 25
"Afternoon Sleep," 4, 32
"Amazed By an Accumulation of Snow," 117
"Andrew Jackson's Speech," 44, 56
"As the Asian War Begins," 59
"Asian Peace Offers Rejected Without Publication," 59–60
"At a Fish Hatchery in Story, Wyoming," 106
"At a March against the Vietnam War," 58, 59, 61
"August Rain," 108
"Black Pony Eating Grass," 119
"Bouquet of Roses, A," 124, 128
"Busy Man Speaks, The," 44, 52, 57, 65

Index 159